SETTLING SCORES

SETTLING SCORES
The Media, the Police & the Miners' Strike

EDITED BY
Granville Williams

CAMPAIGN FOR PRESS & BROADCASTING FREEDOM
2014

To the memory of
Geoffrey Goodman, Industrial Correspondent; Martin
Jenkinson, Photographer, and two militant miners, Joe
Owens and Richard Clarkson.

Settling Scores: *The Media, the Police & the Miners' Strike*
Edited by Granville Williams
Published on 30th anniversary of the Miners' Strike 1984-1985 by
Campaign for Press & Broadcasting Freedom 2014

www.cpbf.org.uk
ISBN: 978-1-898240-06-8

Design and production Roger Huddle
Printed by Russell Press, Nottingham

CONTENTS

Acknowledgements : *9*

Thirty Years On : *11*
         Granville Williams
The Cabinet Papers: Misinformation and cover-ups : *22*
         Nick Jones
The Enduring Story : *34*
         Paul Routledge
The Media Barrage : *41*
         Pete Lazenby
Setting the Record Straight: Inside Out on Orgreave : *53*
         Granville Williams
The Cabinet Papers: Thatcher and the Police : *64*
         Nick Jones
No Roadblocks to Orgreave : *77*
         Ray Riley
Push Ahead On All Fronts: Orgreave Truth and Justice Campaign : *86*
         Granville Williams
Reporting the Next Battle: Lessons from Orgreave : *95*
         Tony Harcup
From Orgreave to Wapping: The Real Enemy Within : *106*
         John Bailey
The Shadow of the Strike: Brassed Off : *116*
         Julian Petley
A Tale of Two Strikes : *125*
         Granville Williams
Last Words : *135*
         Brian Lewis

Contributors : *138*

SETTLING SCORES:

Acknowledgements

This book went from an idea to print in four months. That is in large measure due to the professionalism of the people who have contributed chapters to it. I want to thank them all but in particular Nicholas Jones who alerted me to some of the significant disclosures in the Cabinet papers on the miners' strike. His conversation with me was the spark to produce the book.

Many thanks also to Roger Huddle for his positive support and work on the design and printing of the book. My wife, Sue, also provided invaluable support proofreading and, as always, thanks to Barry White, the tireless national organiser for the Campaign for Press and Broadcasting Freedom (CPBF).

This book is published by the CPBF whose close association with the miners' strike was documented in *Shafted*, published by the CPBF on the 25th anniversary of the strike in 2009. The CPBF, active around the issue of the right of reply and challenging media bias during the strike, published *Media Hits the Pits* in 1985.

I'm sure there will be many other books published for the 30th anniversary of the strike but I want to mention one particularly: *Images of the Past: The Miners' Strike* which contains the photographs of the late Martin Jenkinson, the official Yorkshire NUM photographer during the 1984-85 strike. *

There is one unintended gap in the book. In November 2013 Maxine Peake's play *Queens of the Coal Age* was broadcast on BBC Radio 4. It tells the story about the four miners' wives – Anne Scargill, Dot Kelly, Elaine Evans and Lesley Lomas – who occupied Parkside Colliery, Newton-le-Willows, in an attempt to save the remaining pits from closure in 1993. It was a reminder of the inspiration, resilience and vital role of Women Against Pit Closures (WAPC) during the strike and afterwards. A chapter on WAPC was commissioned for *Settling Scores* but unfortunately the author could not complete and it was too late to make other arrangements.

Tony Harcup's chapter in *Settling Scores* uses documents obtained from the BBC under Freedom of Information. Tony sent me one document which he didn't use in his chapter, a briefing on *Media Hits The Pits* sent to the BBC Assistant Director General (ADG) Alan Protheroe.** What struck me, reading the internal BBC document, was that the points we made in the pamphlet still remain relevant today. Thirty years on the issues thrown up by media coverage of the miners' strike and those to do with media reform remain inextricably linked.

* Mark Metcalf, Martin Jenkinson, Mark Harvey, *Images of the Past: The Miners' Strike*, Pen & Sword Books

 ** The document can be read at: *www.cpbf.org.uk/settling scores*

GW2014

Thirty Years On

Granville Williams

On 3 January 2014, the day the cabinet papers dealing with the miners' strike up to July 1984 were released, I was asked the question on a local BBC radio programme, "Why are you bothered about all this? Move on, it all happened 30 years ago." There were so many injustices perpetrated during the epic 1984-85 struggle, so many brutal political decisions taken that affected, and continue to affect, the lives of tens of thousands of former miners, their families and communities, so many cover-ups, that the question should be reversed: "How can you *not* be bothered?"

Four events prompted the production of this book, just five years after *Shafted* was written to mark the 25th anniversary of the strike. (1) The first was the report of the Hillsborough Independent Panel (HIP), produced after two and a half years' work, in September 2012. There are many parallels between what happened at Hillsborough on 15 April 1989 when 96 women, men and children died in the crush, and the subsequent process of misinformation and distortion by the media, South Yorkshire Police and politicians, and the role played by these same agencies in the miners' strike five years before.

On 15 April 2009, at the 20th Anniversary Memorial of the disaster organised by the Hillsborough Family Support Group (HFSG), the then Secretary of State for Culture, Media and Sport, Andy Burnham, addressed 30,000 people at Anfield, home of Liverpool FC. The sheer tenacity, determination and staying power of the HFSG led Andy Burnham to announce the Government's intention to effectively waive the 30-year rule withholding public records to enable disclosure of all documents relating to the disaster. This paved the way for the Hillsborough Independent Panel (HIP) to be established by the Home Secretary, Alan Johnson. This Panel produced an accurate picture about what happened on that fateful day and subsequently. (2) The report is worth reading in full. For example, one of the untruths widely disseminated in the media was that drunken Liverpool fans played a central role in causing the disaster, but after detailed analysis it concludes: "There was no evidence to support the proposition that alcohol played any part in the genesis of the disaster and it is regrettable that those in positions of responsibility created and promoted a portrayal of drunkenness as contributing to the occurrence of the disaster and the ensuing loss of life without substantiating evidence." (3)

Five years before, media coverage of the miners' strike and the headlines, photographs and film footage presented a relentless portrayal of picket line violence. The media portrayed the miners as the perpetrators of this violence, but what is suppressed by this distortion was the violence unleashed on the miners. The Justice for Mineworkers Campaign points out, "During the strike 20,000 people were injured or hospitalised (includ-ing NUM President Arthur Scargill), 200 served time in prison or custody. Two miners, David Jones and Joe Green, were killed on picket lines, three died digging for coal during the winter and 966 were sacked." (4)

SETTLING SCORES:

Two chapters in the HIP report are especially relevant to issues we explore in *Settling Scores*: Chapter 11 *Review and alteration of statements* and Chapter 12 *Behind the headlines: the origins, promotion and reproduction of unsubstantiated allegations.*

The official report into the disaster, the Taylor Report of 1990, was clear that the main reason for the disaster was "the failure of police control" and Lord Taylor concluded his criticism of South Yorkshire Police (SYP) by describing senior officers in command as "defensive and evasive witnesses" who refused to accept any responsibility for error. He pointed out, "In all some 65 police officers gave oral evidence at the Inquiry. Sadly I must report that for the most part the quality of their evidence was in inverse proportion to their rank."(5)

Chapter 11 of the Independent Panel goes into forensic detail tracking the changes made in police statements. A team of SYP officers and a solicitor were involved in this and 116 statements were amended to remove or alter comments unfavourable to SYP. It points out, "Examination of officers' statements shows that officers were discouraged from making criticisms of senior officers' responses, their management and deficiencies in the SYP operational response: 'key' words and descriptions such as 'chaotic' were counselled against and, if included, were deleted." (6)

Chapter 12 is devastating in the way it traces the widespread dissemination across broadcast and print media (tabloid and broadsheet) of "unproven and unsubstantiated allegations" which persisted for years in public perceptions of the disaster. As the severity of the disaster became apparent on the day, SYP Match Commander, Chief Superintendent David Duckenfield, told a falsehood to senior officials that "Liverpool fans had broken into the stadium and caused an inrush into the central pens thus causing the fatal crush. While later discredited, this unfounded allegation was broadcast internationally and was the first explanation of the cause of the disaster to enter the public domain." What is clear is that SYP in the days after the disaster disseminated a distorted, emotive and sensational version of events which was repeated by local, regional and national newspapers and the broadcast media.

On 19 April 1989, four days after the disaster, *The Sun* newspaper published a front-page story under the banner headline, 'THE TRUTH', alleging that Liverpool fans had assaulted and urinated on police officers resuscitating the dying, stolen from the dead and verbally and sexually abused an unconscious young woman. This was the front page which got national and international prominence. Less prominently, and often with a lesser degree of certainty, other regional and national newspapers published similar allegations. The piece was created by the bullying, foul-mouthed paper's editor, Kelvin MacKenzie. During the miners' strike the paper, a strident cheerleader for the Thatcher government, was often challenged by the printers over its crude, hostile coverage of the dispute. The battles raged over the 'right of reply' and most notably over the MINE FUHRER headline and picture which the print workers refused to touch. The *Sun* appeared on 15 May 1984 with a blank front page and the message: 'Members of all the *Sun* production Chapels refused to handle the Arthur Scargill picture and major headline of our lead story. The *Sun* has decided, reluctantly, to print the paper without either.'

The day after the HIP report MacKenzie gave his 'profuse apologies' for the front page claiming he was misled by 'authority figures' and had believed a 'senior police officer and a senior local MP were making serious allegations against fans in the stadium'. In fact MacKenzie was warned by one journalist who said, "We've got to be really careful with this stuff. These are allegations we're reporting." But things had changed at *The Sun* – there were no printers left to challenge such a scurrilous front page. All of Murdoch's newspapers were printed at Wapping after he sacked 6,000 print and production workers in January 1986 and, apart from 100 journalists, the 'refuseniks', the rest had gone to Wapping. By 1989 Mackenzie was so dominant at the paper that the only person who could control him was Murdoch, and he wasn't around. The responsibility for the front page, displaying all of MacKenzie's deep-seated prejudices, was his alone. Hillsborough campaigner Trevor Hicks, who lost two daughters in the disaster, branded MacKenzie's apology 'too little, too late', calling him 'lowlife, clever lowlife, but lowlife'.

Documents disclosed to the Panel show that the allegations were filed by White's News Agency, a Sheffield-based company. They were based on meetings over three days between agency staff and several police officers, together with interviews with Irvine Patnick MP and the South Yorkshire Police Federation Secretary, Paul Middup. A further document records a meeting in Sheffield of Police Federation members on the morning of the publication of the controversial story in *The Sun*. Paul Middup confirmed that 'putting our side of the story over to the press and media' had been his priority.

The Panel, however, reached different conclusions and "found no evidence among the vast number of disclosed documents and many hours of video material to verify the serious allegations of exceptional levels of drunkenness, ticketlessness or violence among Liverpool fans. There was no evidence that fans had conspired to arrive late at the stadium and force entry and no evidence that they stole from the dead and dying. Documents show that fans became frustrated by the inadequate response to the unfolding tragedy. The vast majority of fans on the pitch assisted in rescuing and evacuating the injured and the dead." (7)

The Media, the Police & the Miners' Strike

On 12 October 2012 the Independent Police Complaints Commission (IPCC) announced its investigation, the biggest independent review of the police ever conducted. By December 2013 the investigation had identified a total of 240 officers whose statements may have been altered and interviewed 143. Thirteen police officers refused to be interviewed. The IPCC is sifting through a vast amount of information which will be for the new inquests into the 96 deaths at Hillsborough which begin in March 2014, 25 years after the tragedy.

The determination and tenacity of the families and supporters of the Hillsborough victims means at last that 2014 might be the year that the real truth about the events on that day, and afterwards, is finally revealed.

The second spur to produce *Settling Scores* was the revelation in a BBC Yorkshire and Lincolnshire regional current affairs programme *Inside Out*, broadcast on 22 October 2012. A young BBC journalist, Dan Johnson, who had good connections with the NUM and miners in South Yorkshire, presented the programme. In the programme's introductory section, Toby Foster made the direct link between the evidence uncovered by Dan Johnson about the 'doctored' police statements after Orgreave and suggested they 'could have led to the culture which five years later on would see the cover-up at Hillsborough'. What the programme revealed was that SYP senior officers deliberately moulded the statements of police officers so that they could prosecute arrested miners for the serious charge of riot which carried a potential life sentence. The programme was well-received but also gave a focus to bitter and long-standing feelings amongst miners and former miners and their supporters about the role of the police at Orgreave, and more broadly during the year-long strike.

Joe Owens, a former Scottish miner, now sadly dead, put it well:

The image of the thin blue line was replaced with that of the beefy paramilitary with the thick black truncheon and riot shield. Illusions of the police as just another emergency service were literally beaten out of miners and their families in scenes of quite sickening brutality. (8)

The programme spurred a group of people to set up the Orgreave Truth and Justice Campaign (OJTC). Since its first meeting on 8 November 2012 it has built up strong support and momentum.

The third stimulus for this book was the death and funeral of Margaret Thatcher in April 2013. A deep chasm was exposed between those who celebrated her life and those who loathed her politics and the suffering her policies inflicted on millions of working people as the shipbuilding, steel, engineering and mining industries were savagely contracted.

'Deindustrialisation' was the clinical economic term for a process which wreaked havoc, misery and despair in communities across the manufacturing and industrial regions of South Wales, Scotland, the Midlands and the North of England. For the survivors of this brutal economic and political process the funeral was a spur for celebration.

The band Chumbawamba broke up in 2012 but on 8 April 2013 the CD *In Memoriam: Margaret Thatcher* was sent out to the people who had been pre-ordering since they announced online in April 2009 that the memorial disk was "already recorded, pressed and ready to go." The band promised the album would be sent out on the day of Margaret Thatcher's death, so that fans could "rest easy in the knowledge that you've put a down-payment on a small and perfectly-formed segment of the celebrations." In a final message on their website they stayed true to the subversive, combative, cheeky spirit that summed up the band's music:

She's not been gone more than a few hours, and already the national media have cranked into gear and begun the blandly respectful eulogies – at their most critical they seem to be only able to say: 'She polarised opinion … what's certain is how much of an impact she made on Britain … etc etc

Twitter set off at a pace with a thousand 'Ding Dong the Witch is Dead' messages only to be followed by a slew of bleeding heart liberals bemoaning the fact that people were daring to celebrate someone's death. Pah! Let's make it clear: This is a cause to celebrate, to party, to stamp the dirt down. Tomorrow we can carry on shouting and writing and working and singing and striking against the successive governments that have so clearly followed Thatcher's Slash & Burn policies, none more so than the present lot. But for now, we can have a drink and a dance and propose a toast to the demise of someone who blighted so many people's lives for so long.

If we must show a little reverence and decorum at this time, then so be it. Our deepest sympathies go out to the families of all Margaret Thatcher's victims. (9)

Goldthorpe in the Dearne Valley, South Yorkshire, is where the poorest parts of Barnsley, Rotherham and Doncaster join. The *Barnsley Chronicle* carried a report of the celebrations in Goldthorpe of Thatcher's funeral on 17 April 2013: "Up to 2,000 people and media from across the country descended on Goldthorpe on Wednesday as a symbolic 'funeral' where an effigy and coffin labelled with the word 'scab' were set alight to mark Margaret Thatcher's death." The report quoted former miner Mark Cresswell of Thurnscoe, who worked as a ropeman at Goldthorpe Colliery for 15 years. He said, "Apart from when my children were born, this is one of the best days of my life. Goldthorpe was a proper mining village and she ruined communities like ours." (10)

The anti-Thatcher celebrations enlivened a former mining village which normally has a depressed air, with many houses boarded up and whole streets being demolished. But Goldthorpe was not always a depressed area. In the 1980s there were three pits around the village, and miners' wages boosted a thriving local community. What broke Goldthorpe, and many other villages surrounding it, was the Tory pit closure programme of the 1990s. Communities were broken up, drug use soared, crime became a serious issue and poor health a major concern. In December 2013 Britain's first "social supermarket" opened in Goldthorpe. It provides food and damaged goods to poor people at around one third of the normal cost.

The publication of the Cabinet papers provided the final spur to produce this book. It was a telephone conversation with Nick Jones, the former BBC Industrial Correspondent, who was researching the Cabinet papers late in 2013, which alerted me to some of the revelations contained in the material on the miners' strike. What the Cabinet papers do is give the lie to the convenient smoke screen created at the time around the role of the government, and particularly Mrs Thatcher, in the strike. We now know for definite what we always suspected - that she mobilised all the forces of the state to take on the miners, was an active interventionist in both the preparations for the strike, the day-to-day conduct of her ministers during the strike, cajoling the police to take a tougher stance against striking miners and subverting the role of local magistrates to ensure that miners were convicted during the strike.

Thirty years on, the fallout from Thatcher's vindictive policies remains toxic. The coal mining economy of the UK was destroyed between 1985-1993 and nothing significant put in its place. During the cold spell in winter 2013 40% of Britain's energy needs were met by coal yet we have the absurdity of UK coal-fired power stations burning coal from Russia, the USA or Australia whilst only three deep-mine pits still exist in the UK: Hatfield and Kellingley in Yorkshire and Thoresby in Notts.

Public utilities – telecoms, coal, gas, water, electricity, railways – were privatised with the alluring but absurd prospect that we could all become part of a 'shareholding democracy' as Thatcher proclaimed she was giving 'power to the people'. However, the bizarre outcome is that huge swathes of these vital services and infrastructure are beyond our control. Take electricity supply - UK firms are absent from this essential service. E.ON of Dusseldorf, RWE of Essen, Iberdrola of Bilbao, the state-owned French company Electricité de France, better known as EDF - these are some of the companies that now control the supply, and price, of the electricity we consume.

The assault on trade unions by Thatcher and the free market economic policies pursued by hers and successive governments tipped the balance of power decisively in favour of employers and the super-rich. Recession and austerity policies have driven down real wages for working people, jobs are increasingly short-term, low paid and often on zero hours contracts. An economy shaped by full employment, strong trade unions and rising real wages has been replaced by one with a small number of highly paid jobs and millions of badly paid jobs.

There is a sense now that, after 30 years, the strike and the sacrifices which the miners, their families and communities endured, and the principled defence of jobs and communities were part of a bigger battle, but one that it was right to fight. To modify the words of the French author, Albert Camus, writing about the Spanish Civil War: "...men and women learned that one can be right and yet be beaten, that force can defeat spirit, that there are times when courage is not its own reward." (11)

SETTLING SCORES:

Notes

(1) *Shafted: The Media, the Miners' Strike and the Aftermath*, CPBF, 2009

(2) http://hillsborough.independent.gov.uk/repository/report/HIP_re-port.pdf

(3) Ibid p179

(4) The National Justice for Mineworkers Campaign at http://www.justicefor mineworkers.org.uk

(5) Lord Taylor, *Hillsborough Stadium Disaster Inquiry report*, January 1990

(6) HIP, p339

(7) HIP, p367 ·

(8) Joe Owens, *Miners 1984-1994: A Decade of Endurance*, Polygon, 1995 p8

(9) http://www.chumba.com/index.php

(10) *Barnsley Chronicle*, 'Goldthorpe protest from the ground,' 19.04.2013

(11) The full quote is: "It was in Spain ... that men learned that one can be right and yet be beaten, that force can defeat spirit, that there are times when courage is not its own reward. It is this, no doubt, which explains why so many men, the world over, feel the Spanish drama as a personal tragedy." Albert Camus (1913-1960) was a French novelist. The above quote is taken from the preface to *L'Espagne Libre* (1946)

The Cabinet Papers:
Misinformation and cover-ups
Nicholas Jones

CABINET PAPERS FOR 1984 released by the National Archives provide a gripping account of the secret steps taken
by the Prime Minister, Margaret Thatcher, as she micro-
managed the government's authoritarian response to
what the trade union movement has acknowledged was
the most critical industrial dispute of post war Britain.

Arthur Scargill's claim throughout the year-long miners'
strike that the National Coal Board chairman Ian MacGregor
had a secret plan to close 70 pits with the loss of up to 70,000
jobs has been proved correct. Cabinet records for 1984 have
revealed that within a month of becoming chairman
MacGregor was advising the government that he intended
to close as many as 75 pits with the loss of 64,000 jobs.

Margaret Thatcher ordered there should be total secrecy about the existence of MacGregor's personal target
for closures. She had been warned by Downing Street officials that under no circumstances should his plans be revealed to the public. So effective was the subsequent cover-up within Whitehall that MacGregor's 75-pit closure
list was never mentioned again in the cabinet papers nor
was it ever referred to during the year-long pit strike.

Because there was no record of MacGregor's true intentions in government documents which related to the coal board, Mrs Thatcher had no hesitation in authorising an advertising campaign to tell the country that Scargill was lying to his members when he claimed MacGregor's intention was to butcher the coal industry and shed 70,000 jobs.

Later, at the height of what became Britain's longest and most violent industrial dispute, the Prime Minister gave her personal approval to a letter in MacGregor's name that was sent to every miner's home. In it the coal board chairman said he could state "categorically and solemnly" that Scargill's claim that 70,000 jobs were at risk was "absolutely untrue."

When the strike began on 6 March 1984 – and then for the duration of the dispute – the NCB insisted that it wanted to close only 20 pits with the loss of 20,000 jobs, a closure rate that the National Union of Mineworkers always argued was far below what the chairman had planned for.

Cabinet records, released under the thirty-year rule, have revealed the full extent of government misinformation during the strike: MacGregor had in fact outlined his personal hit list for pit closures at a private meeting with Peter Walker, Secretary of State for Energy, six months before the start of the dispute. Several days later at a meeting in Downing Street held on 15 September 1983, Walker gave Mrs Thatcher a detailed report on MacGregor's proposals.

A cabinet office note of their conversation revealed that MacGregor "had it in mind" for the three years of 1983-85 that "a further 75 pits would be closed"; the first 64 closures would reduce the workforce by 55,000 and the next 11 would secure a further manpower reduction of 9,000.

His proposed rate of closures would almost immediately have devastated the marginal coalfields, as the secret document makes clear: "The manpower reductions would bite heavily in particular areas: two-thirds of Welsh miners would become redundant, 35 per cent of miners in Scotland, 48 per cent in the north east, 50 per cent in South Yorkshire and 46 per cent in the South Midlands (which included the whole of the Kent coalfield)."

Mrs Thatcher and the three cabinet ministers who knew of MacGregor's secret plan (Nigel Lawson, Chancellor of the Exchequer, Tom King, Secretary of State for Employment, and Peter Walker) would have realised that it would have been a political disaster for the Prime Minister if it had ever emerged that MacGregor had told the government as early as September 1983 that he wanted to close 75 pits.

Scargill had claimed as far back as November 1982 that the NCB had prepared a closure hit list. Public confirmation of its existence would have allowed the NUM president to have accused MacGregor and Thatcher of having been caught lying to the miners and to the country.

Secret – not to be photocopied

Cabinet papers show Mrs Thatcher agreed that no record of Walker's report on MacGregor's plan should be circulated. Six days later in a note to the Prime Minister, Peter Gregson, deputy secretary at the Cabinet Office, advised that because the chairman's plans were so "sensitive" there should be no further written record of what had been said; future estimates of closures and job losses should be referred to by way of "a short oral briefing."

Only one copy was made of the original document mentioning 75 pit closures. At the top of the three-page manuscript is the instruction: "Secret - not to be photocopied or circulated outside the private office." A handwritten note in the right hand corner states: "typed by Lillian, seen by MCS, P Gregson, FERB, one copy made and given to Sir R Armstrong (cabinet secretary)."

Mrs Thatcher's papers include further guarded references to MacGregor's plans for "accelerated pit closures" including notes of another three pre-strike meetings; each of these documents names the typist who would have been one of only a handful of people who knew what MacGregor had in mind.

21 September 1983: Peter Gregson note to Thatcher: "I suggest a short oral briefing...in the absence of written material...the best way would be for the Prime Minister to have further meetings of the small group who met on 15 September."

31 October 1983: Meeting to brief Thatcher: "Walker should be invited to give only the barest background on closures". (typed by Jean, No 1 of 1 copy, not to be copied).

12 January 1984: "The Secretary of State for Energy discussed with the Prime Minister today the plans for closing uneconomic pits...MacGregor wished to raise the target for reduction (from 28,000 over two years) by 16,000 to 44,000." (typed by Monica, only one copy).

18 January 1984: Peter Gregson note to Thatcher: "No ministerial discussion of the NCB's closure strategy since the unrecorded talk you had with the Secretary of State for Energy and the Chancellor of the Exchequer last September...MacGregor disposed to accelerate the rate of closures...this is a highly sensitive matter."

19 January 1984: "The Prime Minister held a meeting today... MacGregor had concluded the run-down ought to be accelerated. This would imply the loss of 45,000 jobs over the next two years...the Chancellor agreed that the rate of closures be accelerated...the PM said that the objective of a more accelerated run-down of coal capacity was accepted." (typed by Rosemary, only one copy)

From cover-up to campaign of misinformation
Cabinet records have also revealed how closely Mrs Thatcher was personally involved in a calculated cam-

paign of misinformation. She personally approved a letter which flatly rejected Scargill's claim that MacGregor intended to "butcher" the coal industry; it stated that the NCB was seeking "20,000 voluntary redundancies", not the 70,000 claimed by the NUM.

The letter was delayed for a week after she asked for a further redrafting and it was finally sent on 21 June 1984, three and a half months into the strike. MacGregor accused the NUM leadership of having "deliberately misled" miners by claiming the coal board intended to do away with 70,000 jobs and close down around 86 pits:

> If these things were true I would not blame miners for getting angry or for being deeply worried. But these things are absolutely untrue. I state categorically and solemnly. You have been deliberately misled.

Three drafts of the letter are included in Mrs Thatcher's papers together with a note from her private secretary Andrew Turnbull discussing the options for submitting another draft; he also warned of the "dangers in substituting another text."

One of the drafts showed that key words were heavily underlined by the Prime Minister; one sentence underlined twice included the line that even if the NUM leadership kept the dispute "going indefinitely" there could be "no victory" however long the strike lasted. Continuing the strike would not result in an "NUM victory" because "in the end everyone will lose – and lose disastrously."

If Mrs Thatcher had at any time doubted her resolve to pursue what became a fight to the finish with Arthur Scargill, the underlined words serve as a reminder that she saw a victory for her government as the only possible outcome.

The "enemy within" – no slip of the tongue

Four months into the strike, when a potentially disastrous dispute in the docks had opened up a second front against the government, the Prime Minister rallied Conservative MPs with her infamous pronouncement that she was ready "to fight the enemy within."

Her war-like declaration was no slip of the tongue: her cabinet papers disclose how she had been fired up to mount a "war of attrition." She was convinced the task of defeating the "extreme left" of the British trade union movement was as great as that of regaining the Falkland Islands. With military precision she secretly ordered the build-up of nuclear and oil-fired generation of electricity to ensure indefinite endurance of power supplies and then bought off sympathy strikes in the docks and on the railways in order to ensure that Scargill was isolated and ultimately defeated.

Her assertion on 19 July 1984 that striking miners were the "enemy within" mirrored the bellicose language adopted by her closest advisers, who included the former Conservative minister John Redwood, then head of her Downing Street policy unit. Mrs Thatcher's conviction that she was in a fight to the finish with the NUM had been strengthened the day before by a private letter of support from the US President Ronald Reagan:

Dear Margaret, In recent weeks I have thought often of you with considerable empathy as I follow the activities of the miners' and dockworkers' unions... My thoughts are with you...I'm confident as ever that you and your government will come out of this well. Warm regards. Ron.

Next evening, addressing a private meeting of Conservative backbenchers, she declared that she had no intention of giving in to the "industrial muscle" of striking miners who were responsible for "violence and intimidation like a scar across the face of the country":

We had to fight the enemy without in the Falklands but we must also remember to fight the enemy within.

Her language that evening mirrored what she and

Downing Street insiders had been saying. At cabinet that morning, on being informed of the breakdown the previous evening of the latest negotiations between the NCB and the NUM, she told ministers the government was entering "a new phase in the dispute" and they had to devise new ways to "reinforce the pressures on striking miners to return to work."

"Encouraging a war of attrition"

A position paper prepared by her policy unit had set out the strategy to be adopted: the "extreme left" aimed to destroy her government and John Redwood urged her to return to her original strategy of "encouraging a war of attrition" to get the miners back to work. "Any fudged formula over uneconomic pits which allows the pace of pit closure to be slowed and the level of subsidy to increase is defeat...There is only one thing worse than presiding over industrial chaos, and that is giving in to the use of industrial muscle for unreasonable ends."

Redwood's advice was dated 13 July and headed "secret, sole copy". The five page document had been heavily underlined by Mrs Thatcher; his warning against giving in to "industrial muscle for unreasonable ends" stood out, having been underlined three times.

In her memoirs, *The Downing Street Years*, Mrs Thatcher says she was "enormously relieved" that the negotiations with the NUM broke down on 18 July because it denied Scargill the chance to "claim victory." From then on her tactic was to get striking miners to realise "they had no hope of winning and a return to work would begin."

Two of her policy unit's key proposals that July were to play their part as the dispute unfolded. Redwood advised use of the law against secondary picketing and to "make an attack on the Yorkshire NUM funds." In the event both strategies were pursued as the strike progressed: working miners went to court to challenge Scargill's repeated declaration that the strike was "official" and it was their legal action which eventually resulted in the sequestration of the NUM's assets.

Dock strike "deliberately engineered" to support NUM
Mrs Thatcher's determination to mount a "war of attrition" against the NUM leadership had been preceded the day before by encouraging news for the ministerial group dealing with the miners' strike. Nicholas Ridley, Secretary of State for Transport, had reported "some promising signs" of a possible settlement to an unexpected dock strike which had been triggered when workers at Immingham, who were not registered dockworkers, had loaded lorries with iron ore bound for the British Steel Corporation at Scunthorpe.

Immediately the dock strike began Mrs Thatcher told the cabinet it was "clearly desirable" to resolve the dispute as soon as possible because the government's priority was to defeat the miners' strike. She was even firmer at a later meeting of the ministerial group handling the two disputes: the priority was to "settle the dock strike as quickly as possible in order to allow the government to concentrate on winning the miners' strike."

Ministers were instructed to reassure employees in the ports that the government had no intention to "alter or abolish" the dock labour scheme which provided guaranteed employment for 13,000 dockers, of whom 4,000 were surplus to requirements; Mrs Thatcher believed the dockers enjoyed "extra-ordinary privileges." Her tactics paid off: two days after Ridley's report on "promising" talks between the two sides, the strike was called off.

She was advised that the dispute in the docks had been deliberately engineered by two leading officials of the Transport and General Workers' Union, Alex Kitson and Walter Greendale, who were said to be anxious to redeem their union's "promises of support for the miners' strike."

There was a second but far less effective dock strike in September 1984 which was triggered by the berthing and unloading at Hunterston of the bulk carrier *Ostia* which the local dockworkers had refused to handle in support of striking miners; the *Ostia* was carrying coking coal urgently needed at the Ravenscraig steel works.

Mrs Thatcher's tactical skill in preventing an extension of the miners' dispute to other key industries had been tested earlier in the year by a threatened rail strike. Again the Prime Minister had been warned that the two key union leaders involved, Jimmy Knapp of the National Union of Railwaymen and Ray Buckton of the train drivers' union ASLEF "would prefer to mount industrial action in order to support the NUM."

When the threat of a rail strike was first discussed by cabinet on 8 May Mrs Thatcher said it was "particularly vital from the point of view of endurance to avoid a combined coal and rail strike." A week later the cabinet agreed to increase British Rail's pay offer from 4.3 to 4.9 per cent in order to "clinch a settlement" so as to "maintain as far as possible the isolation of the miners from the effective support of the rest of the union movement." The following week the unions accepted the offer and the strike threat was lifted.

Only one "game plan": defeat of Scargill

As the picket lines strengthened in the early months of the dispute, and as it became obvious that the NUM would only agree to the closure of loss-making pits if their coal reserves were exhausted, Mrs Thatcher's advisers urged her time and again to escalate the dispute in order weaken Scargill's support.

The advice of her policy unit was often couched in

war-like terminology. There was only one "game plan": defeat of Scargill. Here was confirmation that her promise to "fight the enemy within" had been made in deadly earnest; her tactics increasingly reflected the tone if not always the detail of the secret guidance she was being given:

Redwood (13 July): "You cannot follow a strategy of encouraging a war of attrition ...and a strategy of trying to find a fudged formula...go back to the original strategy of a war of attrition, where the perceived way of the strike ending is for miners to go back to work."

Redwood (29 August): "Speedier use of stipendiary magistrates and of legal processes so that pickets can see their comrades being prosecuted and punished quickly for criminal offences...Examining the possibility of mounting a conspiracy charge against union leaders inciting pickets to violence."

Redwood (7 September): "The coal industry is comprehensively bust. The activities of the NUM and the attitude of many NCB managers have contrived to ruin a potentially profitable resource industry. Where nature has endowed our country generously, predatory unions have succeeded in turning a national asset into a national liability. Experiments could be made with giving bad mines to miners, along with a substantial capital sum if they were prepared to try and make a go of it themselves...offering the worst mines to miners along with a dowry, would have presentational advantages."

Redwood (21 September): "Encourage NCB to extend its threat of dismissal to all those not only convicted of criminal damage against Coal Board property, but also those convicted of serious offences against persons on picket lines or NCB property."

Redwood (3 October): "It is vitally important the NCB should sack any miner convicted of violence against fellow NCB employees or property."

Peter Warry (26 October): "We need to regain and retain the initiative...following the NACODS settlement...eliminate the idea that further NCB concessions are just around the corner...place more cards in our hand by upping the stakes...withdraw assurances of no job losses for those that do not return."

Warry (9 November): "The screw needs to be gradually tightened...start talking about the possibility of withdrawing capital investment promises in non-working areas."

Warry (13 November): "The lengthy strike is causing inexorable geological destruction on faces and whole pits...must at some stage make it impossible for the NCB to continue to guarantee that no striker will ever face compulsory redundancy."

Notes

(1) In her memoirs, *The Downing Street Years*, Mrs Thatcher paid tribute to Redwood and Warry; she said Redwood became the "extremely effective" head of her policy unit in 1983.

Redwood defended his role as Mrs Thatcher's adviser when he was interviewed on the *Jeremy Vine Programme* on Radio Two (3 January, 2014). He confirmed that Ian MacGregor had secretly wanted to close 75 pits – "far more than was sensible"– but believed he had fulfilled his own personal ambition to encourage miners to have a go at seeing whether they could make a go of uneconomic pits. In 1995, when Secretary of State for Wales, he said he "helped the miners of Tower Colliery to take over their pit, which they operated under their own direction for many years."

(2) BBC television archive footage for the 1984-85 strike provided a vivid flashback – and a graphic illustration –of MacGregor's deliberate misinformation about pit closures.

Arthur Scargill: "We don't want to see pit closures and a run down in manpower levels bearing in mind they have a hit list of 70 pits and a reduction in manpower in mind of about 70,000."
John Tusa (presenter): A further reduction of 70,000 jobs over two years? Can you deny that?
Ian MacGregor: "I know of no place where that has ever been discussed. We have nothing like that on our agenda."
BBC *Ten o'clock News*, 3 January 2014.

The Enduring Story
Paul Routledge

It is the story that just doesn't go away. The main characters are dead, retired or long forgotten, but the story of the Great Strike for Jobs has a life all of its own. Not a living legend, but a narrative that has not yet reached a conclusion – if it ever will.

That was brought home forcibly on 8 April 2013, when Margaret Thatcher died and the mining communities of South and West Yorkshire, Durham and elsewhere erupted in spontaneous celebration.

The gaiety over a life ended was condemned as tasteless and demeaning by those who didn't understand it. "Don't speak ill of the dead" was rolled out in defence of the Iron Lady. But she had little good to say about the men and women of the pit villages when she was alive, and now it was their turn.

Anticipating the event, I had written a long feature article about Thatcher and the strike for the *Daily Mirror*. It was already 'in the can', as they say. You can do that with new technology. But, as is their wont, my newsdesk wanted something more topical, something happening on the day. "Go and talk to some miners," they demanded.

"Ex-miners" I corrected them, there being so few of

the real thing, and even fewer among them who took part in the year-long strike. By now it was early afternoon, and I travelled post-haste from my base in Keighley to Moorthorpe, on the eastern fringe of Wakefield Metropolitan District. My first port of call was the Empire Workingmen's Club, where the Frickley colliery NUM branch used to meet in 1984-85. Incidentally, that's why they were known derisively among the young Turks of the pit as 'the Empire Gunners' – "because you're allus gunner do this and you're allus gunner do that!"

There were no young bloods in the bar. How could there be? The pit, a million-tonne a year high-performer that once employed 4,000 men, shut in November 1993, with devastating economic consequences for the village of South Elmsall where most of the workers lived. But there were veterans of the strike, downing pint after pint in honest revelry.

I had with me a photographer from Leeds, Ben Lack, and we talked and he snapped away through the afternoon. Greg Whitehurst, 69, said: "The Tories always hated the working class. They hated us, and we hated her. She should have died thirty years ago." Johnny Stones, 75, struck a pensive note. "I'm sorry for those who cannot be here today," he said, "those who passed away before she died." Alas, Greg died only eight months after Thatcher.

In the Brookside Social Cub down South Elmsall High Street, they played Judy Garland's "Ding Dong, The Witch is Dead!" time after time at ear-splitting volume. One lad danced up and down the bar, a danse macabre of celebration. As I wrote in the *Daily Mirror*: "In this corner of England, there was no grief. It was cabaret time." In Goldthorpe, just down the road, they burned an effigy of Thatcher. In Co Durham, I attended a party at Easington Colliery Miners' Welfare, as much a celebration of endurance as of their tormentor's demise.

The Media, the Police & the Miners' Strike

But all this was simply a curtain raiser on what was to come in January 2014, when the National Archives began to disgorge documents about the strike kept secret under the 30-year rule. Only then did the full scale of Tory deceit come into plain view.

This story ran in all the papers and on the television news. It was a double-page spread in the *Daily Mirror.* Some right-wing papers, like the *Daily Mail,* sought to play down the revelations. *The Times* went big on Thatcher's "top secret plan to catch miners smuggling suitcases full of Soviet cash" and ignored the "hit list" of 75 collieries due for closure. But this was a proper story, and it couldn't be ignored outright. It ran for days, giving fresh impetus to the Orgreave Truth and Justice Campaign set up in November 2012 in the wake of revelations in Dan Johnson's BBC *Inside Out* programme. This documentary exposed the way in which police officers had been coached to give the "right" evidence to support charges of riot brought against 95 picketing miners, charges eventually dismissed.

Publication of the strike papers also got me back into the BBC studios for Look North. The programme makers were obviously keen to observe 'balance'. They felt the need to make some kind of nod towards the other side. I was told to expect a question hostile to the conduct of the dispute, and I had a ready-made answer. In 1981, in his office in 222 Euston Road, Arthur Scargill, newly-elected president of the NUM, gave me a list of more than 40 pits at risk of closure.

The list was culled from internal Coal Board computer printouts of colliery financial performance. This was the 'Scargill hit list', and I published it in The Times on 23 August 1981. The NCB denied that there was a central 'hit list' of planned closures, as shutdowns were a matter of local negotiation. South Wales director Phil Weekes went so far as to denounce it as a 'miss list', though all 46 were closed.

So was born the notion of a 'hit list', which became a central element in Scargill's campaign to halt closures. It also seems to have resonated within the Coal Board and government circles, because ahead of the conflict NCB boss Iain MacGregor privately briefed Thatcher and her minister of his plan to close 75 pits. This was not the unofficial 'Scargill list' – it was the real thing and almost twice as long – and it was not disclosed until the laws governing declassification of state papers required it to be published.

By then, of course, its propaganda value had greatly diminished. If Scargill had been able to flaunt this official programme in the face of the media when the dispute was getting under way, it might have made all the difference to miners in so-called moderate areas who thought their pits were safe, unlike the militant coalfields of Scotland, Kent and South Wales. In reality, it made no difference. The pits of the 'working miners' were closed just as rapidly as those where the strike had been strong.

It has to be kept in mind, of course, that newspapers are a private sector industry, with highly-political (invariably Tory) proprietors and/or shareholders whose primary interest is in profit, not printing the truth. That's why the papers could not bring themselves to give due weight to the exposure of Thatcher's lies. Even after 30 years, this is still a toxic issue for the Establishment. Many of the combatants at the highest political level are dead, but some are still mouldering on the red leather benches of the Lords, and the inheritors of their power feel a bounden duty to uphold the official version of events.

So, faced with a request from Labour for an apology for the lies, David Cameron refused and threw the demand back in the faces of the Opposition with a demand for an apology from Scargill for "the appalling way in which he led that union." This line didn't get much of a show, though it was the lead item on the politics and economy page of the *Yorkshire Post*. But it showed yet again that the story that wouldn't go away still hadn't gone away. Scargill himself is still box office, even though he's been retired for ten years or more. A second BBC *Inside Out* programme broadcast in Yorkshire in January 2014 sought to establish what had happened to the very large sums of money that had been donated to the NUM during the strike. In a sense, it was a re-run of the Lightman Inquiry set up by the union itself in the wake of the dispute. The investigation, which had a hurried look about it, produced little that was new, apart from highlighting the activities of the Paris-based International Miners' Organisation to which the NUM was affiliated and paid tens of thousands in subscription fees for no very obvious purpose.

There was no killer fact, but the programme did disclose that Scargill had sought to buy his 'council flat' in London's Barbican, which he had occupied for many years, under Thatcher's "right to buy" legislation. This story was buried in the detail, and it was several days before the media cottoned on. It was then given the full treatment, as might be expected, in a hostile press exulting in the 'hypocrisy' of the former NUM president.

The treatment of the story emphasises yet again the biased, sometimes crude, nature of the media. Thatcher died in a private suite in the Ritz paid for by a rich admirer, but this passed virtually unnoticed in the press. It's all right when the rich do what the rich have always done, but 'double standards' in the Labour movement are held up to ridicule. Hence the ballyhoo about rail union leader Bob Crow taking a holiday cruise to Brazil on the eve of a strike by his members on the London Underground against – yes, you've guessed it, just like the miners – closures and job losses.Is there any point in using the media, when its abuse is so persistent and so flagrant? Michael Dugher, Labour MP for Barnsley East who grew up in the shadow of Yorkshire Main colliery with family and friends on strike, obviously thinks so. He contributed to the *Yorkshire Post* a cogently-argued article describing his attempt to wring an apology from the Tories and secure publication of the documents relating to police/government relations during the strike. (1)

Headlined, "Without truth, there is no justice for the miners", he wrote of the lasting sense of injustice in the coalfields "both because of the damage those events inflicted and because of the failure to hold to account those in power at the time." Labour's 'Justice in the Coalfields' campaign, he admitted, cannot undo the damage that was done, "but we can shine a light on what happened."

Exactly so. The men and women who lived in mining communities through the great ordeal of 1984-85 know what happened, because it happened to them.

But the world at large has a short memory span. The public remembers that something very hard took place 30 years ago. They sometimes see TV footage of picket line scenes, and of Scargill speaking to mass meetings of strikers. But they rarely see or read about the real issues of the dispute, or the long-lasting impact it had on the people whose lives it changed forever. Much of the media doesn't want them to know.

However, the unexpected clarity and force of the National Archive revelations can alter that perspective. It has provided an opportunity to move away from the trivial coverage of Scargill's phone rental or the funding of his private car to the big issues that are still unresolved: the ministerial instructions to police chiefs to adopt a "more vigorous interpretation of their duties" which led to a clampdown on the movement of pickets into the working coalfields, the fitting-up of miners in the 'Battle of Orgreave'. And so on and so on.

That's why the Orgreave Campaign and Labour's

Coalfields Campaign deserve our support, and why the message they bring to a wider audience must be heard. It took decades for the Hillsborough Campaign to succeed, but succeed it did in its prime objective of finding out what really happened. As every year passes, it gets harder to get the truth, but that's no reason to stop trying. And that's why it's imperative to use every possible media outlet to galvanise the truth process.

Our media, particularly the press (with the exception of the *Morning Star*, but that's a whole other story), is flawed. Sometimes fatally so. But without Dan Johnson's BBC film about the dodgy police tactics at Orgreave, I doubt if the campaign for justice on that single-issue topic would have got off the ground. Without the publicity given to the Thatcher 'hit list' lies, Labour's campaign for justice in the coalfields would not have been possible. Don't expect too much, but never give up. As Channel 4's Paul Mason points out, "The truth on paper still has the power to shock."

Amen to that.

Note

(1) Available at: *http://www.yorkshirepost.co.uk/news/debate/ columnists/michael-dugher-without-truth-there-is-no-justice-for-the-miners-1-6418507*

Pete Lazenby

I BECAME INDUSTRIAL REPORTER on the *Yorkshire Evening Post*, then the biggest regional newspaper in the biggest coalfield in Britain, in 1974.

My first personal experience of media hostility towards the National Union of Mineworkers (NUM) – or more particularly Arthur Scargill – occurred on the island of Jersey. At the time Arthur was President of the Yorkshire area of the union. Bitter battles were being fought within the NUM between left and right. Lancastrian Joe Gormley was National President of the union, and enjoyed a cosy relationship with the chairman of the National Coal Board (NCB), Sir Derek Ezra.

Despite that relationship the miners had staged two national strikes, in 1972 and 1974, bringing power cuts and, in the latter case, the downfall of Edward Heath's Tory Government. Joe had unsuccessfully attempted to postpone the 1974 strike.

The result of the strikes was that the annual conferences of the NUM became a 'must' for media coverage. The conferences' decisions had an influence on the future of the UK. Coal provided over 70 per cent of the country's electricity. The miners set the pace for pay and working conditions in other industries. So the ranks of Fleet Street's industrial correspondents, press agencies, TV and radio, attended the NUM's annual conferences.

Jersey may seem a strange location for anything involving the NUM. The nearest coal mine at the time was over the water in Kent. But Jersey was twice the venue for the union's annual conference – once in the 1970s after the 1974 strike, and once in 1981 as Joe's personal choice because it would be his last as President as he was due to retire. Joe liked his little luxuries. He enjoyed majority support on the union's national executive committee, despite the presence of a powerful left influence which included respected Scottish communist Mick McGahey who was national vice-President, and fellow Scot and general secretary Lawrence Daley.

Arthur Scargill, already a national figure as leader of 65,000 Yorkshire miners, opposed the choice of Jersey as venue for the union's annual conference, arguing that the event should take place at a venue accessible to miners, ie on mainland Britain, and preferably close to the coalfields. Jersey is of course a holiday and tourism island. It has luxury hotels, and the union's national executive committee stayed in a fine one. Most of them saw nothing wrong with that. "Nowt too good for the workers," as they say. I won't argue the point. Up to 1974, many of the Jersey hotel staff were French. In April 1974 came the Portuguese revolution, and the downfall of the Salazar fascist dictatorship. The change led to an influx of cheap Portuguese labour to the island of Jersey. Hotel owners snapped them up. When the NUM conference took place in Jersey, the hotel in which the NUM executive stayed was served by Portuguese workers – waiters, maids and the rest. They lived in appalling conditions – sheds built of breeze blocks, with holes in the walls which passed as windows, but with no glass or frame. They slept on mattresses on the floor. There was no furniture. Arthur found out about the living conditions and was horrified. Here was the miners' leadership enjoying the hospitality of a fine hotel, while the people serving them every day were living in the hotel grounds in shocking conditions.

He decided to speak out. He did so, publicly, and the media latched on to the story. The hotel vehemently denied his statements about the workers' living conditions.

Jersey was served by its own TV station, Channel TV, which invited Arthur to be interviewed about his claims. I remember the day – it was a Wednesday, which was always a 'half day' at the NUM conference. Conference business finished at lunch-time on the Wednesday, leaving delegates, and in many cases their wives, to enjoy an afternoon of relaxation, which isn't difficult in a place like Jersey.

At the time the editor of the *Yorkshire Miner* newspaper was Maurice Jones. Over the years I worked closely with Maurice. We became friends. Maurice said that Arthur had obtained visual evidence of the Portuguese workers' living conditions to prove his case when he was interviewed on Channel TV. A sympathetic photographer employed by the NCB had been recruited, and had taken pictures of the living conditions – which incidentally I went to see myself.

By this time the story had gone viral, as we say today. The interview was to be sent to the UK national ITV network by Channel TV. There were also political ramifications to the story, involving the wider trade union movement. Hotel staff on the island were organised by the Transport and General Workers' Union. Back on the mainland Arthur was seen to be trespassing on TGWU territory by taking up the hotel workers' case. There were suggestions that the TGWU would withdraw its customary support for the election of NUM delegates to the Trades Union Congress.

So a lot was hanging on the Channel TV interview with Arthur, and on his proving his case about the Portuguese workers' living conditions. The NCB snapper who had gathered the photographic evidence had given Maurice the film. The problem was getting it developed. Remember, this was the mid 1970s, pre-computer days. Photographic film had to be developed in a darkroom, by someone who knew what they were doing. I was given the job of finding somewhere to get the film developed. This was around 1pm. Arthur was due at the TV studio at 5.30pm. I was provided with a taxi. In those days you took your holiday snaps to the chemist's to have them developed. It could take a week. Some provided a 24-hour turnaround service. Even that was no use – the photos were needed in a few hours. I was eventually told that the only place with facilities to develop the film in time was Channel TV. So I headed there. I explained the situation at reception, that Arthur Scargill needed the photographs for use in his interview there later that day. A technician was sent for and took the film, promising that the photos would be ready by the time Arthur arrived. I went back to the hotel, told Maurice about the arrangement, and joined the Industrial Correspondents relaxing by the hotel swimming pool.

At 5.30pm Arthur went to the TV studio for the interview. There were no photographs for him. An embarrassed technician said that the film had been 'accidentally over-exposed' during the development procedure. In other words, the evidence which proved Arthur's case had been destroyed. He made the case in the interview – but without the visual evidence which would have made it undeniable. The business community on Jersey is close-knit – hotels, tourist operations, media.

There is no doubt in my mind that the destruction of the photographic evidence was deliberate. I've told this story before, but have never written it down.

Another example of media bias was closer to home. In 1982 transport workers took strike action in support of nurses. The day of action was called for a Monday. Train and bus drivers planned to take part, and public transport was expected to be paralysed. That Monday's *Yorkshire Post* had a front page story telling how workers in their thousands defied the strike and used every means possible to get to work – shared cars, bicycles, taxis. But the deadline for stories in the *Yorkshire Post* was 2am or 4am in the event of a late-breaking story. So it had been written before any of them had even got out of bed.

I mention these cases as a back-drop to what was to come later regarding the media and the miners during and after the 1984-85 strike against pit closures. The appallingly biased media coverage of the strike is well-documented. Along with other journalists I have written about it before in the book *Shafted*. It identified the media's in-built antagonism towards not only the miners, their union and their leaders, but towards all organised labour – a situation which has existed since the very birth of trades unions in Britain, a situation which continues today.

Here's a very small example of how it works. Unions always make 'demands' when asking for a pay rise for workers. Employers always make 'offers'. It's such a simple use of words isn't it? 'Demands' suggest aggression, 'Offers' the kindly response of the employer.

Then there are the union 'barons', as described by much of the establishment Press. Never mind that union leaders are elected democratically by their members. Never mind that no-one ever has a chance to elect a real baron, or any other of Britain's medieval and out-dated aristocracy. As a reporter on the *Yorkshire Evening Post* I rejected the use of such terms in my copy. Unions make proposals for pay rises, not demands. It's a small thing, but important for all that.

One of my first major stories after being appointed Industrial Reporter in 1974 was covering the miners' strike of that year – the one which contributed to the downfall of Ted Heath's Tory Government in the general election that year. One of the problems for journalists like me, journalists who were also socialists and active trade unionists, was the understandable reluctance of many miners, particularly branch officers of the NUM at local pits, to talk to the press. There were around 70 pits in Yorkshire at the time, each with four branch officers: President, Vice-President, Secretary and Treasurer.

46

But I was extremely fortunate. The pub where journalists from the *Yorkshire Evening Post* drank in Leeds was the *Central Station* in Wellington Street. The licensee was Brian Frost, an ex-miner from Sharlston colliery outside Wakefield. The village of Sharlston was an isolated and independent community, built solely to house the pit's 1,000 miners and their families. As was the case with so many mining communities, the pit was Sharlston's economic base. Without it there was no reason for the community to exist.

Social life also revolved around the pit. There was the Kibble club – the local miners' welfare and social club. I was told Kibble was a word meaning 'coal tub'. The club had been called the Kibble because when it first opened the club was tiny. The name stuck, even after the club expanded. Brian Frost had worked at a pit in Featherstone a few miles down the road. He told me that when he transferred to Sharlston he was seen as an 'outsider', and it had taken some time for the Sharlston miners to accept him as 'one of them', even though he was a miner. Final acceptance came when he married into a local family. And not just any family. Wendy had an extended family which had influence in the community. Brian quit the mining industry to enter the licenced trades. He was a tough man. He'd played rugby league and had the face to go with it as a result of the knocks he'd received.

Brian and Wendy kept in close contact with her family in the Sharlston community. During the 1974 strike I talked to Brian in the *Central* over a beer. He and Wendy invited me to visit the Sharlston community with them. Effectively they were to open the door for me, vouch for me. That visit led to the establishment of friendships which continue today. The pit closed in the last raft of closures in 1993. The friendships at Sharlston led to many more in other Yorkshire pits and mining communities, including Kellingley colliery, now one of the last three working deep mines in Britain.

Working with the NUM led to another friendship which lasts today – with Anne Scargill, who, when I first met her, was married to Arthur. Anne knows more than most about the media's treatment of the miners, and in particular of Arthur. She and her daughter Margaret also suffered the media hounding which followed the miners' strike, when sections of the media sought to finish off the job of destroying the NUM and its leaders.

The media's attacks on the NUM's national leaders – notably President Arthur Scargill and General Secretary Peter Heathfield – plumbed new depths, even by the standards of much of the tabloid press. It was the supposedly Labour-supporting *Daily Mirror* which led the attack in 1990, with allegations that during the strike Arthur and Peter had stolen union money to pay their mortgages. That was followed by Central Television's *Cook Report*, with the same allegations. Outright lies of course, as subsequently proved. (1) But it had lasting effects.

Here's how Anne Scargill remembers it:

All hell broke loose with them saying he had stolen all this money. The *Daily Mirror* came out, then the *Cook Report* came out. Here was I, working at the Co-op in Barnsley, and a lot of them thought we had stolen all this money and there was a hell of a lot of hostility towards me from people because of what they were writing in the Press.

That period when the *Mirror* turned on Arthur was one of the worst periods of my life. It was horrible. That *Cook Report* as well. He was a bastard. He knew Arthur was not at home but he was harassing us. We couldn't go out, couldn't go to work or anywhere.

On one occasion the Press even used a local hunt for a murderer to smear the Scargills. The family had security CCTV cameras outside their home in Barnsley. Police asked to see the videos – they were checking all security cameras in the area for sightings of the wanted man, Michael Sams. Police approached Anne. She said the cameras were Arthur's responsibility, and said they should approach him. Anne said:

> They rang Arthur and he told me to give it to them. The *Mail on Sunday* then had a big headline saying Arthur Scargill's wife was refusing to help police in the Julie Dart murder enquiry. One of the police had leaked it.
>
> In the afternoon this police inspector came to see me and apologised. He said, 'I'm sorry, I know it isn't true.' I had said the video was not mine, you will have to ask Arthur. I didn't refuse it. They got in touch with him and he 'phoned me up and told me to give it to them.
>
> Then there was the *Cook Report*. Roger Cook came to our house this particular morning. He had seen Arthur at the gate and Arthur had gone to work. It left me and Margaret to face up to all this barrage of Press. They knew he was not there, but I couldn't go out or come in without they were at you.
>
> When Roger Cook turned up at the door Arthur had rung us from the car to say there was Roger Cook outside and don't go to the door. So I couldn't go to work. Margaret was at Leeds University but couldn't

get out of the house. He kept coming and putting the camera to the windows, shouting outside, so I sent for the police to him.

They came and said there was nothing they could do. The only thing you could do was sue him for trespass. I said to the police well you arrested me in the strike in Nottinghamshire and that was not for trespass and I was only stood outside the pit gates, but you can't do anything with him?

That was the first time he came. The second time he came was at the miners' conference in Durham. I was driving the car up to the conference centre and he was there again. All the time there was this harassment. Every time I went into town I thought everybody was thinking that we had got millions of pounds of theirs. I hated going into town when all this started.

I have to say this: Tony Benn rang me at home a couple of times and told me to get out there, hold my head up high and that true working class people knew it was not true, what they were saying in the Press, and I should not let it get me down.But it was a truly hard period, was that. (2)

The editor of the *Mirror* at the time of the allegations in 1990 was Roy Greenslade. In 2002, I suppose to his credit, he admitted wrong-doing, writing in *The Guardian*:

On March 19 this year the highest court in France, the Cour de Cassation, ordered Roger Windsor, former chief executive of the National Union of Mineworkers, to repay a debt of £29,500. The judgment went unreported in Britain, as did an NUM press release more than a month later that celebrated the court's ruling.

Yet this case - and Windsor's humiliation - deserves the widest possible audience because they are the culmination of a deplorable saga which goes some way to vindicating a wronged man: NUM president Arthur Scargill. Wronged by the press in general, by the *Daily Mirror* specifically and, since I was then its editor, by me.

We journalists seem to find it impossible to apologise for what we have written and I know, sadly, that some old friends and colleagues won't appreciate this *mea culpa*. But lingering embarrassment is far outweighed by my heartfelt delight in being able, at last, to put the record straight by saying sorry.

The apology came too late for the other 'wronged' man, Peter Heathfield. Peter was a man of impeccable honesty and character. The media allegations against him broke him. He eventually descended into dementia. I last saw him at the annual memorial lecture to Davy Jones and Joe Green, two miners killed on the picket lines during the 1984-85 strike. He was a shell of a man and died in 2010.

The media barrage against trade unions and trades unionists continues today. The trade union movement numbered 13.5 million in 1979 when the Thatcher Government came to power. Today membership is six million. It is my belief that the right-wing media – the likes of the *Daily Mail* – will not be satisfied until trades unionism in Britain has been wiped out altogether. Britain has more anti-trades union legislation than any other country in Europe. New shackles are continually being forged. The latest imposes a "gag" on political campaigning, other than by political parties, in the run-up to the next general election. It will prevent trades unions promoting their views on political issues. The House of Lords voted 245 for the legislation, 245 against, meaning that the Government won. It is a shameful, undemocratic piece of legislation. And of course it will not gag the most influential opinion formers in Britain – the media, and in particular, the tabloid press.

Newspaper circulations are falling. Yet the establishment press's collective circulation is still more than 10 million copies a day. Each paper sold is assumed (by those who know about these things) to have at least two readers, meaning that well over one-third of the adult population is potentially being influenced by a mainly right-wing, union-hating, Tory-supporting Press.

The paper on which I now work as Northern Reporter sells less than 20,000 copies a day. The *Morning Star* is the lone, daily, national voice of the labour and trades union movement. It supported the miners in their epic struggle to defend their jobs, their industry and their communities.

A diverse media is vital for democracy. Today's concentration of the vast majority of the press in the hands of a few rich, powerful, right-wing media magnates does not augur well for the future of democracy in Britain.

Here's one final point. Some reporters, in our own small ways, have tried to change the attitudes of a new generation of journalists towards the miners. In my case my links with Kellingley colliery helped. At times of high staff turnover in the 1980s – when there were jobs in journalism to go to - the *YEP* would have several trainee or junior reporters. When the number reached half a dozen or so I would organise an underground visit to Kellingley, to give them a taste of a miner's working life.

Underground visits usually took place on a Saturday when the face was not working, and maintenance work was being carried out, but I arranged the visits for a working day, when coal was being turned, so the young journalists could experience the dust, the noise, the 'violence' of gouging thousands of tons of coal from a seam in the single journey of a coal ripper, not to mention the speed at which the metal cage dropped a quarter of a mile to the pit bottom, the three-mile ride lying on a conveyor belt to the coal face, the stumbling between the 40 or so gleaming metal hydraulic pit props along the quarter-mile length of the face.

One trainee on one of these visits was the son of a former Tory party chairman, and step-son of a Tory Cabinet Minister. After the visit, emerging grimy-faced at the pit-top, he said simply: "Pete, I didn't know."

I hope the lesson stayed with him.

Notes

(1) Seumas Milne, *The Enemy Within: The Secret War Against The Miners*, Verso, 30th anniversary edition, 2014

(2) The section of this chapter quoting Anne Scargill is taken from *Only a Miner's Daughter*, a book I have written jointly with Anne Scargill, telling her life story, which is currently being edited.

SETTLING SCORES:

Setting the Record Straight: *Inside Out* and Orgreave
Granville Williams

> *"We had a very fortunate collision of timing, the right elements being at the right time to bring it altogether and strike a chord."*
> Dan Johnson

Introduction

Sometimes television programmes can catch the mood of the time and stimulate action by individuals and institutions. The BBC *Inside Out* programme on Orgreave which went out in the Yorkshire and Lincolnshire region on 22 October 2012 did just that. The core of the programme was the revelation by BBC reporter, Dan Johnson, that a batch of South Yorkshire Police (SYP) witness statements for miners arrested at Orgreave demonstrated the extent of police fabrication of the evidence.

The programme was aired just one month after the Hillsborough Independent Panel (HIP) report, which triggered a stream of announcements that ensured the behaviour of SYP was rarely out of the news in the weeks following. On 14 September, two days after the panel's report was published, West Yorkshire Chief Constable, Norman Bettison, a SYP chief inspector at the time of the Hillsborough disaster, issued a statement saying fans 'made the job of the police...harder than it needed to be' and then issued a second statement in which he apologised for appearing to partially blame supporters. On 12 October the Independent Police Complaints Commission (IPCC) said it was launching the biggest-ever inquiry into police behaviour in the wake of the HIP report and on 24 October Bettison resigned as chief constable of West Yorkshire with immediate effect. Three weeks after the *Inside Out* programme SYP self-referred their conduct at Orgreave to the IPCC mentioning the programme and naming the reporter Dan Johnson personally in the referral.

54

I first met Dan Johnson at an NUM weekend school in Scarborough in December 2008. I mentioned that I was trying to pin down at which pit the hilarious snowman incident really occurred. Dave Douglass tells it like this in *All Power to the Imagination*:

> The miners of Silverwood, having been told they were confined to six pickets only, built themselves a seventh comrade in the shape of a large snowman, wearing for good measure a plastic policeman's helmet.
> Next morning, Chief Inspector Nesbitt appears on the scene and seeing the jeering miners and their steely eyed companion, ordered the constables to knock it down. This order brought rebellion to the police ranks as PCs declined to, "look so fucking stupid knocking down a snowman". "Very well," shouts the irate Nesbitt, jumping in his Range Rover and charging off to demolish the snowman, as pickets ran laughing for cover.
> Maybe it was a trick of the light, or maybe a twinkle glistened in the icy countenance on the snowman's fixed expression - we shall never know, as the Range Rover made contact and came to a dead stop, smashing front grill, bumper and headlamps and hurling the

shocked Nesbitt into the steering wheel. PCs found excuses to walk away or suppress body-shaking laughter while pickets fell about on the ground with side splitting mirth. The snowman had been constructed around a three foot high two foot thick concrete post!

Dan contacted John Nesbitt, at the time of the strike the SYP chief superintendent who arrested NUM President Arthur Scargill at Orgreave on 30 May 1984. Nesbitt's name was always associated with the story but he told Dan the incident never happened. Nesbitt cited as evidence the fact that the South Yorkshire Police Authority ordered an inspection of all Range Rovers for damage and they couldn't find anything. He conceded, however, that his association with the story caused him some career problems.

Dan Johnson was born in Barnsley. "I grew up with the stories about the strike, took an interest, and always had a sense there was unfinished business there, something had not been told to people's satisfaction," he said. (1) His interest in the miners' strike (he was born half way through it) developed whilst studying for a Geography degree at Leeds University when he was researching energy policy. His dissertation was on the miners' strike, with a focus on police tactics. He also did a couple of articles about pit closures for the student paper. Later, after a post-graduate journalism course at City University, he got work with Radio Sheffield covering the decline of coal mining, the closure of Rossington pit and later Maltby.

Making the Programme

The idea for the programme came from an article by David Conn in *The Guardian*. It made the connection between the SYP behaviour at Hillsborough and the way miners described their actions at Orgreave and other events during the miners' strike. (2) "But Conn had not nailed it," Dan said. "There wasn't any evidence to actually prove it. I was thinking about it and I know the *Inside Out* team were thinking about it separately. It was only when the Hillsborough panel report was published and there was that clear evidence about police statements being changed and the prime minister gave a full apology and announced the steps that would be taken to remedy the injustice that we heard mutterings 'that's not the first time statements were altered by SYP' but again the question was 'how do you prove it – where's the evidence?'"

56   The idea that the statements had been altered sparked a tiny flicker in his mind. For his student dissertation he had spoken to one of the miners who was at Orgreave, one of those charged, tried and acquitted, and he remembered that he had all the statements, not just the ones relating to his own arrest but the ones relating to everybody's arrest. Dan had looked at these way back in 2005-06 for his dissertation, thought them very interesting, a bit of history, flicked through them, and gave them back. But after the Hillsborough report he thought 'that's it' – the former miner had got the evidence and he managed to get in touch with him and obtain the statements.

"There were 120 original statements mouldering away in a garage, quite stained and smelly, but definitely the genuine article, with just one page missing. As soon as you start looking through them you realised the second one is the same as the first one and the third one the same as the second – you start recognising the pattern," Dan said.

He pays tribute to the people he worked with on the programme, particularly the 'very good' researcher, Lucy Smickersgill. "The *Inside Out* team really came into its own, being able to go through the statements, analyse exactly what phrases are repeated and how many times," he said. "They did a cross reference to how many officers had used exactly the same phrases word for word and which force those officers were from. They pieced together an analytical breakdown of how much repetition there was."

The statements also gave the names of the officers. The next task was tracking down the officers named in the statements. Dan recalls the overwhelming impression that the police didn't want to talk about it. Some were very angry about being contacted. One in particular he remembers: "I went round to his house, he lived locally and his wife answered the door, and I just explained what we were doing and asked if he could get in touch. She obviously rang him straight away and he rang me from work as I was driving away: 'What are you doing knocking on my door, interfering with my wife. You've no right. How have you found me? This is absolutely atrocious. I am astounded that the BBC is trying to hunt people down to talk about these issues 30 years on. Disgraceful. No, I do not want to talk about it. Leave me alone - your approach is definitely unwelcome.'"

A few spoke anonymously and a couple were willing to appear on camera and talk about their statements. One in particular described how he was sent into a room and a CID officer came in and said, "Here's the way you start your statement." His claim was that all the CID officer was doing was setting the scene, giving them a generic description of what happened at Orgreave that day, but that he wrote down his own details of the arrests he made.

Although Dan hasn't had any contact with the police officers since he says, "I have a suspicion they may feel regret for being involved now they realise the impact the programme has had."

The other key element for a credible programme involved the former miners whose names were on the witness statements. Some had passed away, but others didn't want to be interviewed. Of the miners contacted it was evenly split between those willing to participate and those strongly against it. "When some of the miners don't want to be involved you start questioning the whole thing then," Dan said. "You think are we actually pursuing a worthy aim here? Having grown up with these stories and hearing that an injustice was done at Orgreave it was a little bit frustrating when you say 'I am trying to highlight this and address it'. I don't know if it was because it was personally difficult to revisit some of this stuff or because they don't think it will achieve anything, or they think so much time has passed and they have so little faith in the system that they want to leave it alone. It was very pleasing in the end that some of those who didn't want to speak to us, when they saw the programme, contacted us to say 'good job, wish I had done'."

The programme fell into place then. "We needed to tell the history of the strike, the key events, and fill in the background to Orgreave for people who didn't know the story. That was enough for us to sell the programme," he said.

The Programme

Dan Johnson's introduction links the two events of Hillsborough and Orgreave: "While Hillsborough resonated around the world, what happened at Orgreave has been left as a footnote in history," he says.

A rapid summary of the key events of the miners' strike up to Orgreave in June 1984 follows, placing events at Orgreave in the context of a previous miners' victory – the closure of the coking plant in Birmingham during the 1972 strike. (3) "Saltley acted as a template for the picketing at Orgreave 10 years later only this time the miners faced a police force and a government determined not to be beaten," he comments. Ten thousand miners were at Orgreave on 18 June with at least five thousand police from many different police forces from across the country, there to stop the miners shutting the coking plant. Dramatic footage of the mounted police charge is interspersed with commentary from Yvette Vanson (who made the powerful *Battle of Orgreave* in 1985), the former Hadfield Colliery miner Dave Douglass and two police officers.

Michael Mansfield represented several miners in the first Orgreave trial of miners held in Sheffield in 1985. In the programme he points out that police video footage of events that day show a completely different picture to the one the BBC and most other media broadcast. The police version was that there had been a violent assault on the police and there had been no choice but to send in the mounted police. But there were also a lot of independent monitors, with notebooks, cameras and one with a movie camera in a tree. Mansfield says, "The police had no idea of the extent to which their unlawful activities were being filmed. Putting the combination of that package together you had a record, an almost unchallengeable record, of a completely different version of events."

Stef Wysocki, a former Derbyshire miner, gives his shocking testimony of his treatment that day when he was arrested: "I hadn't done anything so I didn't think I would get charged. When I was arrested at the top of the hill there were a lot of photos of me with no injuries but when I got to the bottom of the hill I'd got injuries while I was in their custody...Bruises, facial cuts, bleeding. I was marched down the field, both arms behind my back, and when we got to the police line I was banged onto the police shields, they bounced me off, the shields opened and I was punched, kicked, prodded, you name it. I walked in and I was nearly carried out."

When the miners were put on trial in Sheffield the case collapsed in spectacular style after 16 weeks when it became clear the police evidence wasn't reliable. Dan Johnson compares the fabrication of police witness statements at Orgreave and Hillsborough and says that the manipulation of police witness statements at Orgreave appeared to be even more manipulated than at Hillsborough. He cites one example where 31 officers from four different forces used this identical phrase: 'As we stood there in the line a continuous stream of missiles came from the pickets into the police line...there were no shields being used at this point'. He asks, based on the extensive fabrication of evidence in the statements, whether it was the intention of the police to present evidence to support a charge of riot – which carried severe penalties – rather that a public order offence, which would mean a fine.

Vera Baird, who also represented miners at the trial, comments on the behaviour of SYP detectives who told police officers what to write: "You can see in a way that they were trying to set the scenario but what they were actually doing was 'teeing up', perverting the course of justice."

In the final section of the programme Michael Mansfield points to the miscarriage of justice at Orgreave: "Not a single police officer was prosecuted, even the one caught on camera beating a defenceless miner to the ground in one famous case. Not a single police officer prosecuted, not a single police officer even disciplined,"

Mark George, a Sheffield barrister and an independent voice with no previous involvement in the Orgreave case, after analysing the statements, concludes the level of repetition in the statements provided enough evidence for the charge of attempting to pervert the course of justice.

The Impact of the Programme

On the same evening the *Inside Out* programme went out an hour-long special *Panorama* programme was to be shown at 10.35pm investigating what the BBC knew about Jimmy Savile, his actions and the events around the dropping of the Corporation's own *Newsnight* investigation into the subject. The *Panorama* programme led all the bulletins but the Orgreave programme got some good pre-publicity. *Breakfast News, Look North* and *The Guardian* ran it that morning. The *Today* programme and 5 Live ran it as well as local radio stations. Yvette Cooper, Labour MP for the former mining areas Pontefract and Castleford and Shadow Home Secretary, mentioned it in Parliament and said it needed investigation. Lunchtime national news ran it with a plug to watch it. Local papers ran it the next day or later in the week. But the big outcome from the programme was, as Dan Johnson said, "Three weeks after SYP did self-referral to the IPCC and the programme and I were mentioned in the referral so it's pretty obvious what sparked the SYP decision."

He thinks the programme was, "A good example of regional current affairs television, and I don't see that going on anywhere else. The BBC is doing this and is able to shout about it on wider platforms. It is the only place I can see that I could make films like this. There have been cuts to regional news and current affairs but *Inside Out* hasn't lost its capacity to make programmes though they are often now shared more widely across regions."

The programme won the regional O2 media award for Scoop of the Year in May 2013 and the Royal Television Society Best Factual Programme award in June 2013.

Broader Issues

Dan Johnson's Orgeave programme stands out as a good example of regional investigative journalism which makes a difference. However, local and regional journalism, both print and broadcast, have been subjected to huge pressures, particularly since the recession of 2008. These pressures have been due to commercial greed and short-sightedness by regional newspaper groups, successive governments' deregulatory policies which have seen the effective dismantling of ITV's regional structure that sustained vibrant news and currents affairs programming, and the ideological assault on the BBC licence fee in 2010 by the then Culture Secretary, Jeremy Hunt.

Regional newspaper groups up to the 2008 recession were incredibly profitable, but a combination of declining sales, loss of advertising revenue through the economic downturn and increasing Internet competition has led regional newspaper groups to cut jobs, close titles and pursue policies which make it increasingly difficult for local and regional newspapers to fulfil their vital democratic role as local watchdogs. In July 2009 Bedworth, a small former mining town in the Midlands, lost its weekly newspaper, the *Bedworth Echo*. It was one of nearly 50 which its owner Trinity Mirror closed over 18 months in 2008-09. Bedworth became a 'town without news'. In 1972 when Pete Lazenby started on the *Yorkshire Evening Post* (YEP) there were 200 journalists working across the *YEP* and the *Yorkshire Post*. When he left there were 60. In the 15 months up to January 2014 30% of the journalists on the papers were lost. The papers are owned by Johnston Press, one of the big four regional newspaper groups. In February 2014, Newsquest, another of the big-four regional newspaper groups, provoked votes for industrial action by journalists on papers like the *Northern Echo*, *Darlington and Stockton Times* and Bradford *Telegraph and Argus* over an ill-conceived plan to move sub-editing operations of these papers to a central hub 270 miles away in Newport, South Wales. (4)

ITV Yorkshire is a pale shadow of what used to be an independent ITV franchise, Yorkshire Television or YTV, which served the region well. It is now part of a single ITV structure for England and Wales and any sense of a strong journalistic presence in the Yorkshire region has been diminished. The broadcasting regulator Ofcom has allowed ITV to reduce its public service obligations to provide high-quality, well-resourced news and current affairs for all ITV regions. In Yorkshire it means that the

62

single *Calendar* programme at 6.00pm is required to carry more news originating not from the region but from ITV/ITN News in London.

The BBC too is still coming to terms with a shabby, behind-closed-doors deal on the licence fee in October 2010. During 48 hours Mark Thomson BBC Director General, Culture Secretary Jeremy Hunt and the chair of the BBC Trust Sir Michael Lyons agreed to freeze the licence fee until 2017 while taking on £340 million extra spending commitments for the BBC World Service, the roll-out of broadband in rural areas and funding local TV and online services. (5) The consequence of the deal was job losses and a 20 per cent spending cut across the BBC.

If we value our local and regional media we have to speak out in their defence. Journalists, who have no control over the decisions made by top management, show up every day, doing their best to produce good quality reporting. They're often frustrated and even angry at the obstacles placed in front of them. Despite the low pay and high stress of their jobs, they still want to do their best. And at their best they hold local politicians, the police and bullying bosses to account. They are a voice for people angry at bureaucratic incompetence and in support of local campaigns for traffic crossings and swimming baths. As the song says, "You're gonna miss me when I'm gone."

Notes

(1) Interview with Dan Johnson, 24 January 2014.

(2) David Conn, 'Hillsborough and Battle of Orgreave: one police force, two disgraces', *The Guardian*, 12 April 2012.

(3) For my personal recollections of the events at Saltley Gate see 'Forty Years After: What's In A Name?': *http://www.saltleygate.co.uk/*

(4) *The Economist*, 'The town without news' 23 July 2009; *Red Pepper*, 'An industry gutting itself',Feb/Mar 2014; *Press Gazette*, 5 February 2014.

(5) www.nuj.org.uk/documents/bbc-cuts-there-is-an-alternative

The Cabinet Papers: Thatcher and the Police
Nicholas Jones

AFTER ONLY A WEEK OF THE year-long pit dispute Margaret Thatcher had intervened to "stiffen the resolve" of
chief constables whom she believed were failing to provide police protection for those miners who wanted to
report for work. Her cabinet papers for 1984 reveal that
she demanded action after becoming "deeply disturbed"
at the way the National Union of Mineworkers had re-
sorted so quickly to unlawful mass picketing to intimidate those men who had volunteered to work normally.

Within four days of her intervention police were
turning back flying pickets from Yorkshire who were
heading south on the motorway to coalfields in the Midlands and Nottinghamshire. Striking miners from Kent
were being turned back at the Dartford Tunnel.

Mrs Thatcher's impatience at the slow process in the
courts led to repeated interventions. She believed the
impression had been created that the miners' president,
Arthur Scargill, was being allowed to operate "above the
law" in pursuing the pit strike.

The government's top law officers, the Lord Chancellor Lord Hailsham and the Attorney General Sir Michael
Havers, were both urged to exercise their authority after

Mrs Thatcher was told that magistrates in Rotherham and Mansfield were "dragging their feet" in dealing with cases involving pickets arrested for pit head violence.

Two months into the dispute, secret letters from the Lord Chancellor also disclosed private concern within the Nottinghamshire constabulary about the cases being presented to the courts. By May 1984, after over 900 arrests in the Nottinghamshire coal field, Hailsham advised Mrs Thatcher that the Chief Constable of Nottinghamshire had "expressed reservations about the quality of some of the evidence upon which the arrests have been made, and for this reason is not anxious for dates of trial to be fixed too soon."

Later the same day the letter to the Prime Minister was amended. In fact, said the Lord Chancellor, the cause of the concern was that the chief constable was "anxious lest delay causes the quality of the evidence available to deteriorate."

Nonetheless, despite Hailsham's rewording, the revelation that as early as 16 May 1984 a chief constable had privately voiced his concern about the "quality of the evidence" to be presented to the courts could prove highly significant in view of the continuing demands for an inquiry into police conduct during the strike.

In the event, as the chief constable feared, there were months of delay in bringing many of the cases to court and the release under the 30 year rule of the secret correspondence regarding police conduct in Nottinghamshire will inevitably spark comparison with events in South Yorkshire where 95 pickets, who were arrested during the "Battle of Orgreave" for riot and unlawful assembly, were all acquitted after defence lawyers argued that police evidence had been fabricated.

Mrs Thatcher's papers also reveal that her government had extensive contact with the South Yorkshire Police – the force that was not only in command at the "Battle of

Orgreave" but also during the 1989 Hillsborough football stadium disaster, which again is the subject of an ongoing investigation into the accuracy of police statements.

Thatcher demands "more vigorous" police response

Mrs Thatcher's first behind-the-scenes intervention was at a meeting in Downing Street on 14 March 1984, a mere eight days after the start of the miners' strike. Ian Mac-Gregor, the National Coal Board chairman, protested about the ease with which "militants" had succeeded in preventing access for miners who wanted to work; he complained that there had been no arrests.

She agreed it was vital to uphold the law to prevent mass picketing. A second meeting was called because it was "essential to stiffen the resolve of chief constables." Leon Brittan said he was not satisfied with the response of chief officers but he had gone to "the limit of what the Home Secretary could do while respecting the constitutional independence of police forces."

Mrs Thatcher asked for a fuller report to see if the police were "adopting the more vigorous interpretation of their duties which was being sought." Later that day the full cabinet was told police in Nottinghamshire were "exercising their powers to stop coaches carrying flying pickets." But Mrs Thatcher repeated her demand for more "vigorous action": the government should provide chief constables with any assistance they needed "to react with speed and flexibility" before large numbers of pickets were able to assemble.

On first hearing of the concerns of MacGregor and the Secretary of State for Energy, Peter Walker, she admitted that she feared Scargill was about to repeat his success of the 1972 pit strike when flying pickets from Yorkshire succeeded in closing the Saltley coke depot, a setback which eventually forced the then Conservative Prime Minister Edward Heath to concede a 27 per cent pay increase for mineworkers.

Because of her consternation that she too might be defeated by the size and strength of the pickets assembling at pit gates, she considered it "vital that criminal law on picketing be upheld." She had become "deeply disturbed" by the NUM's success within a matter of days in being able to organise flying pickets to stop coal production.

A note of the meeting, written by her private secretary Andrew Turnbull, set out the Prime Minister's absolute determination to thwart Scargill:

Helping those who volunteered to go to work was not sufficient; intimidation had to be ended and people had to be free to go about their business without fear. It was essential to stiffen the resolve of chief constables to ensure that they fulfilled their duty to uphold the law.

Mrs Thatcher's impatience at the failure of the police to do enough to remove the threat of intimidation was even more explicit at the second ministerial meeting. At the start of the week 93 pits were open, but ten where men were willing to work had since closed due to picketing.

Again a note of the meeting left no doubt as to the Prime Minister's frustration: "It was essential for the government to be seen to be upholding the criminal law on picketing...It appeared that the police were not carrying out their duties fully as large pickets were being permitted and few arrests were being made."

Four days after her intervention there was a massive police operation across the motorway network to identify and turn back NUM pickets heading for the pits which were continuing to work in the Nottinghamshire and Midlands coalfields in defiance of the strike.

In news reports next day the Chief Constable of Humberside, who was co-ordinating the operation, denied that the police had become the political weapon of Mrs Thatcher; their job was to ensure "the rule of law" was maintained.

The Media, the Police & the Miners' Strike

"Generous" support for Nottinghamshire police

At another ministerial meeting that week the Home Secretary reported that a total of 7,245 police officers were on duty in Nottinghamshire to keep the pits open; one option considered was the use of military helicopters to take even more police officers to the coalfields to ensure continued protection for working miners.

In another move later in the month the Prime Minister told the Home Office to respond in "a sympathetic and generous way" towards the additional cost of providing police support for the working miners of Nottinghamshire.

As the number of arrests increased Mrs Thatcher started to congratulate the police on their efforts to protect working miners. A month into the strike, after more than 100 arrests at Creswell colliery in Derbyshire which had been besieged by 1,000 pickets, the Prime Minister said it was "totally wrong and false" for the NUM to accuse the police of being heavy handed; it was a slur on the police for the "superb way they have kept open a man's right to go to his place of work unmolested."

But eight months into the strike a secret Home Office report admitted the police tactic of intercepting pickets on motorways and main roads could have been counterproductive. Stopping them at police boundaries and turning them back from likely sites of trouble might merely have diverted them to other destinations. The problem was, once diverted, there was "no longer such good information" about where they were likely to go.

Magistrates "dragging their feet"

Nonetheless as the arrests mounted for breaches of the peace, obstruction and criminal damage, so did Mrs Thatcher's intolerance of delays in the courts. Four months into the strike, at a series of ministerial meetings on 16 July 1984, the Attorney General criticised the slow progress: magistrates had dealt with only 20 per cent of the 2,800 cases which were pending.

The two main courts, Rotherham and Mansfield, were "dragging their feet" over the appointment of stipendiary magistrates. Mrs Thatcher urged the law officers to look at ways of "speeding up the process" because the failure to deal with indictable offences was giving the impression that "Scargill and his union were above the law as far as the dispute is concerned."

By late August her frustration with the courts prompted direct intervention. Sir Michael had recommended that Lord Hailsham should "remind, if necessary enforce", the magistrates' courts to accept stipendiary magistrates. He set out the steps that had been taken: "Today the ring round of the clerks to the justices has started...the un-co-operative courts have now been warned that a stipendiary will be appointed if the backlog justifies whether they request it or not."

But time and again the cabinet papers contain references to Mrs Thatcher venting her anger at the failure to reduce delays in the courts:

Cabinet meeting, 13 September: Home Secretary reported a total of "rather more than 6,000 arrests but about 5,000 of the resulting court cases remained to be tried." Prime Minister said delays were a cause for concern – "violence appeared to go undeterred; both the government and the legal system risked being brought into disrepute... the government might make it known that the cause of the delay was at local level and challenge the magistrates' committees to be more co-operative."

Cabinet meeting, 20 September: Prime Minister said the strike had lasted for some six months but "relatively few cases of alleged violence or other serious offences" had been brought to trial. The Home Secretary should ensure magistrates' courts did "not impose artificial or unreasonable delays" on the relevant committal proceedings.

Ministerial group, 25 September: Home Secretary said Lord Chancellor would see what could be done "to expedite trials."

Ministerial group, 27 September: Home Secretary said of more than 7,000 arrested, some 1,200 had now been tried.

Cabinet meeting, 18 October: Home Secretary said inroads had been made into the backlog of cases..."over 50 people had now been sentenced to terms of imprisonment."

Home Office note to Prime Minister, 11 November: 7,700 arrests to 6 November; 3,400 cases dealt with; and "almost 3,300 cases outstanding, including many of the worst offences."

Ministerial group, 13 November: Attorney General said backlog of cases had been "greatly reduced" in the magistrates courts, where nine stipendiaries had been provided. Prime Minister called for discussion on "further ways of reducing what still appeared to be unacceptable delays in trying the most serious criminal cases."

Secret support for South Yorkshire Chief Constable

Among the de-classified documents are notes and letters which reveal how Mrs Thatcher and government law officers forged a close working relationship with South Yorkshire Police, the force that faced the most violent picketing during the 1984-85 miners' strike.

Four months into the strike, the South Yorkshire Chief Constable, the late Peter Wright, was given secret authorisation to go on incurring the additional cost of bringing in police reinforcements to help ensure the resumption of coke deliveries during what became known as the "Battle of Orgreave". Mrs Thatcher told the Home Office to give the South Yorkshire force "every support"; in the corner of one document is her hand-written note asking: "Can we provide the funds direct?"

Wright's tactics in commanding the massive police operation to prevent mass picketing outside the British Steel Corporation's coking plant at Orgreave had been condemned by the South Yorkshire County Council and its Labour majority on the South Yorkshire Police Authority which both supported the National Union of Mineworkers.

After the county council passed a resolution calling for the Orgreave coke depot to be closed, the police authority withdrew Wright's discretion to spend up to £2,000 without prior authority. Leon Brittan and Sir Michael Havers took swift action on 3 July to support Wright and set in train a series of secret contingency measures. Confidential correspondence reveals that the Home Secretary proposed that the Treasury Solicitor should immediately make funds available if required by the chief constable.

Wright intended to prepare a local RAF barracks to accommodate police support units needed to reinforce South Yorkshire Police, ready for the re-opening of Orgreave the following Monday. Brittan advised Mrs Thatcher: "We need to move quickly in this way to forestall public speculation that police operations against the dispute will be hampered, or even that the Armed Forces would have to be brought in instead."

Next day, at a ministerial meeting in Downing Street, Sir Michael said he was seeking a judicial review of the police authority's decision. He was also considering whether to seek an injunction to prevent the authority from suspending its chief constable on "improper grounds".

At cabinet, Brittan reported that police operations to control picketing in South Yorkshire had continued to be successful and the following day, as a result of the application for a judicial review, the authority was ordered to suspend its action against the chief constable pending a further court hearing.

Brittan feared that other police authorities under political control sympathetic to the miners' strike might copy South Yorkshire's tactic. The previous month the Merseyside Police Authority had attempted to prevent its chief constable from sending reinforcements to help prevent mass picketing.

In backing the steps taken by the Home Secretary and the Attorney General, Mrs Thatcher said the South Yorkshire Chief Constable should be given "every support". It was most important that police authorities should not be allowed to take action to "interfere with the operational judgement of chief constables in policing the dispute."

Peter Wright was supported again by the Home Secretary in September after his "left-wing" police authority said it intended to "phase out all horses and some dogs" from the South Yorkshire force, a proposal which Brittan said would result in the authority failing to carry out its statutory responsibilities to maintain "an efficient police force." After an escalation that same month in picket-line violence outside the Maltby pit, Wright assured Brittan that his force required "no additional resources."

As the mass picketing intensified during the early weeks of the strike, the Prime Minister ordered a full review of the effectiveness of both police tactics and enforcement of the criminal law. In June 1984 the Attorney General assured Mrs Thatcher the criminal law was sufficient "to embrace all the mischiefs" which had manifested themselves during the dispute.

Despite criticism of the way pickets had been turned back on main roads and motorways, Sir Michael was confident of the government's position on "well-established principles of common law" regarding the power of the police to stop people travelling to the scene of an actual or apprehended breach of the peace.

He thought there was no doubt the efforts of the police had achieved "a greater degree of success" than in any similar law-and-order confrontation. The key to this success had been the "deployment of thousands of additional police officers in the areas concerned"; chief constables had not lacked the manpower they thought necessary.

According to the Home Office statistics on police reinforcements up to June, about 4,000 additional officers were being supplied on a daily basis.

Eight months into the strike the Home Office prepared a report on the effectiveness of the mutual-aid reinforcements to control mass pickets. Officials monitored police operations at the Rossington pit in South Yorkshire and Woolley colliery in West Yorkshire. The report revealed that the forces most sought-after to supply reinforcements were from non-metropolitan areas in the south of England such as Cambridgeshire, Norfolk, Surrey, Avon and Somerset and West Mercia.

> Metropolitan police support units were valued in violent confrontations but at other times, and these occasions were more frequent, their attitudes were thought to be harder for local people to identify with and so perhaps more likely to lead to an increase in tension. The casual approach of metropolitan police support units had been a surprise to these forces which had not the same experience of public order problems being treated as everyday occurrences.

Note

So far the National Archives' release of cabinet records containing Mrs Thatcher's papers relating to the miners' strike extends to 20 November 1984. Her documents and papers for the remainder of 1984, and the lead-up to the miners' return to work on 5 March 1985, are due to published in August 2014.

However, other files which contain minutes of meetings of the full cabinet and minutes of meetings of the ministerial group dealing with the miners' strike (known as MISC 101) do extend for the full calendar year of 1984.

When journalists were briefed on the contents of the 1984 cabinet papers which were released on 3 January 2014 under the 30 year rule, they were told by staff at the National Archives that all files relating to the advice and activities of the Security Service (MI5, MI6, GCHQ etc) have been removed and are not being made available to the public.

Nonetheless a few tantalising references have escaped the censor's net. A note has to be included indicating when a file has been removed and the date of such removals sometimes gives a clue as to the significance of the missing document.

For example, a note dated 15 October 1984 by Andrew Turnbull, who was Mrs Thatcher's private secretary, which was sent to her principal private secretary Robin Butler, stated: "The security service is not my expertise but I expect the Prime Minister will be disappointed by this minute which indicates some improvement in police procedures but little action by the security service. What do you think?"

The only other clue is another note stating that a document from Brittan (Home Secretary) to PM dated 15 October 1984 has been retained under the Public Records Act (and has not been published). Similarly a note from Butler to Taylor dated 16 October 1984 was also retained.

Again documents are missing or not properly explained when references are made to the visit to Libya by the NUM's chief executive, Roger Windsor.

Peter Walker, Secretary of State for Energy, gave Mrs Thatcher a report on Windsor's visit to Libya at a meeting of the ministerial group on 29 October 1984. He said there was evidence this visit had been "concealed" from members of the NUM executive and that "personnel of Libyan state organisations had been involved in making and paying for travel arrangements."

A note on the line ministers should take if asked by the news media stated: "Clear that a vast spectrum of public opinion condemns Scargill's activities with the Libyan authorities. The government shares this deep concern. It is time for the voice of sanity to be heard once again on the NUM national executive."

Four days later – on 2 November 1984 –Robin Butler, the Prime Minister's principal secretary, sent a note to the cabinet secretary, Sir Robert Armstrong, that stated that Mrs Thatcher was greatly concerned by the contents of the Box 500 report. "She has asked if you could consider urgently whether there is any way in which these developments could be prevented, whether by denunciation or otherwise." (Box 500 is the term the civil service uses to identify secret reports from the Security Service).

Armstrong replied on 5 November that there were "no powers which could be used to prevent the transfer of funds from abroad to the National Union of Mineworkers." But once received by or paid to the account of the NUM, such funds would be of "considerable interest to the sequestrator."

Armstrong's reply to Mrs Thatcher then set out, but with no specific detail, the steps being taken by the Security Service:

Those concerned are exercising vigilance for any indication or movement of NUM staff to foreign destinations which might be for the purpose of collecting consignments of notes. If we become aware of any movements of funds to the beneficial account of the NUM through banking channels, they can be discreetly reported to the sequestrator.
Mr Scargill has already admitted to being in contact with and receiving assistance from Soviet and other East European trade unions. Steps are being taken to prompt journalistic inquiries of Mr Scargill as to

whether he or other members of the NUM have been in contact with the Soviet or any other East European embassy to discuss or receive the provision of aid.

There is further correspondence in the files relating to the action taken by the Foreign Secretary Sir Geoffrey Howe to discover the role of the Soviet government in transferring funds from Soviet miners to the NUM. A note dated 20 November stated that it "would be most unlikely that the Soviet miners' union could have been given access to convertible roubles without express Soviet official permission."

But again there is only a tantalising hint as to action being taken in secret: a document from "Mann to Butler dated 18 November 1984 with attachment" has been removed from Mrs Thatcher's files and closed to the public, in this case, for 40 years.

No Road-Blocks to Orgreave

Ray Riley

I WAS AWARE THAT THE FIRST scab lorries had left the coking plant at Orgreave on Wednesday 23 May 1984, and on the Thursday before the 18 June around a thousand of us had picketed the plant, with Arthur Scargill himself joining our ranks on the Sunday calling for a mass picket of the works.

I wasn't always sure where we would end up picketing as the union often had a strange way of deploying its activists. So when I arrived at the Frickley Miners' Welfare that morning to be given our destination of the day - be it Orgreave or the agonising journey to scabland in the Nottinghamshire coalfield or even to some unknown and rather obscure coal import terminal on the Humber estuary - it was at the welfare that a rather solemn looking branch secretary informed us that today's picket would indeed be Orgreave and that today was going to be a massive demonstration of strength by the union with pickets coming from as far afield as Kent, Wales and Scotland.

The date 18 June 1984 had an eerie expectation to it. It was different to most days on the picket line where there would be plenty of shoving and pushing, occasional boredom, a few bricks hurled here and there in retaliation to police heavy handedness, choice language, snarling German shepherds, continually being stopped en route to a picketing destination by the police and the usual spectacle of 'Maggie's Boot Boys' frog-marching away lads, who, more often than not, happened simply to be in the wrong place at the wrong time.

What I wasn't prepared for, however, were the graphic events that would unfold in which the state literally declared martial law on striking miners. Whilst I was at Orgreave I became witness to the events, including the beatings, the numerous arrests, the near misses, the military precision of police operations, the suspension of habeas corpus and, at one point, myself and others physically dragging a policeman off a young lad then 'legging' it out of harm's way. The narrative of the strike cannot, however, be understood simply in terms of the unlawful mass arrests of pickets, or the gratuitous acts of violence perpetrated by the police that day, or the cynical decision by the legal system to prosecute the men arrested under the archaic criminal law of 'riot', or even the unwillingness of the media to report and chronicle fairly the events of that day.

Orgreave didn't happen by chance, was not conceived by Arthur Scargill's strategies of engagement, nor was it an aberration involving a 'one-off' mass conflict that would pit the striking miner against an overwhelming force of militaristic proportions. Orgreave, on the 18 June 1984, was an altogether more nefarious affair, as the uninterrupted journey from South Elmsall (where Frickley Colliery was based) proved as the police waved car after car off the M1 slip-road and allowed us to initially amass at the top of a hill overlooking the coking plant. Perhaps at this point the proverbial penny should have dropped as to the ease with which we were allowed through to our destination.

With the benefit of hindsight it was as cynical as it was calculated; part of a premeditated and well executed trap for the police to put into practice its arsenal of tactical crowd control techniques that had been secretly developed over the preceding years.

First, a reminder of the events leading up to the 18 June and why Orgreave was targeted in the first place by the union. A sudden decision by the local British Steel management to increase the supply of coking coal to their Scunthorpe works, above the quantity already agreed with officials of the Iron and Steel Trades Confederation (ISTC) and the National Union of Mineworkers, was carried out. Was it conceivable that the Scunthorpe management had observed the successful use of lorry convoys used to smash through the miners' picket lines at Ravenscraig in Scotland? Besides, this decision, like all major moves against us, was invariably taken only with Downing Street approval, *The Observer* noting on the 3 June that British Steel had approached the government the month previous for the go-ahead. The questions must therefore be asked: Was there a connection between this decision to increase coking coal supplies from Orgreave? And why was a mass picket involving several thousand striking miners able to take place?

I recall us pulling up very near to the local Asda which looked down onto the plant and in the distance we could see the M1 motorway with vehicles of all shapes and sizes travelling along in a northerly direction. The day was fine and sunny with Asda doing a roaring trade in coca-cola, snacks and, of course, cigarettes. It wasn't that someone gave a signal to begin the slow descent down the hill and towards the increasing swell of police lines, it was simply a realisation that the scab lorries carrying furnace coal to the plant would soon be exiting the M1 for their short journey to the plant.

In September 1981, a new approach had been adopted

by members of the Association of Chief Police Officers (ACPO) at their private annual conference in Preston where they met in emergency session to discuss the theme of public-order. Three forces with particular expertise were invited to address the event. Two of them were familiar from previous years. The London Met reviewed the events of the summer of 1981 when England experienced major riots across a number of cities resulting from inner city deprivation and racial tensions, fuelled by a deep distrust of the police and authority, and gave a candid assessment of the inadequacy of police operations to contain disorder. The four main riots occurred in Brixton, London; Handsworth, Birmingham; Chapeltown, Leeds, and Toxteth, Liverpool. The Royal Ulster Constabulary gave a presentation of crowd control techniques they had adopted and refined for use in the Northern Ireland Troubles. Then came the turning point. A new force, outside of the United Kingdom, was invited to describe measures it had perfected to contain public disorder. It brought to ACPO more than 20 years of experience of suppressing riots and uprisings and, moreover, was expert in coping with far greater levels of street violence than occurred in the United Kingdom. (1)

The force in question was the Royal Hong Kong Police. This was an almost unprecedented occurrence involving colonial processes, as John Alderson, Chief Constable of Devon and Cornwall, commented that the usual practice was for developed traditions to be exported to the colonies, not the other way round. At the ACPO conference, Richard Quine, Director of Operations of the Royal Hong Kong Police, had been invited to attend and outline these colonial methods for dealing with public order. Outside of police circles, this visit was kept secret. In 1982, the Hong Kong Commissioner himself, Roy Henry, began attending ACPO meetings in the UK, his status being one of participating observer.

SETTLING SCORES:

The conference made an important decision. They set up a working party to review British riot control tactics in the light of experience of other countries and came up with a programme of action. Its title was, 'The Community Disorder Tactical Options Inter-Force Working Group'. One of the Chief Constables who was present at the conference has given an account of the thinking behind it:

> We had learned some hard lessons about the training of police officers. Forces in the main urban areas were already pretty well trained in the use of the Police Support Unit (PSU), the tactics of crowd control, the use of shields to form cordons and so on. But the forces that came to our aid from rural areas were not as well trained and it became obvious that in order to respond to emergencies, everyone had to be trained to the same standard, with the same tactics. Otherwise it was just confusion...That meant that we had to have a national training package, a national manual on which to work. So ACPO set about devising one. (2)

Immediately following the visit by Richard Quine, ACPO asked if their specialists in public order could visit Hong Kong to see these brazen colonial techniques in practice. Roy Henry was more than happy to accommodate them, and the group studied the Hong Kong force during their exploratory tour of foreign police tactics in many countries. The language used to describe this new police approach was striking, with Henry talking about the projection of police units in an efficient, effective and formidable manner which creates an atmosphere in the riotous mobs of apprehension and awe which could come close to fear. Chillingly, Roy Henry went on to say that if the police get it right, a crowd will scatter: "They will run like the dickens!"

Quine then proceeded with the recommendations of the formation of an elite squad of police officers who would be committed to continuous training over a period of 10 weeks, in a concentrated burst of tactical exercises covering all kinds of disorder, crowd control and riot suppression in particular. Quine further showed the British police a handbook containing all of Hong Kong's expertise in the art of public order management. It was its manual of internal security instructions. (3) Attendance at ACPO conferences between 1982 and 1985 gave Roy Henry a privileged view of the system and tactics adopted for use in the UK and enshrined in the Public Order Manual produced in 1983.

82

Within 2 years they had prepared a massive volume of paramilitary and other related manoeuvres called 'The Public Order Manual of Tactical Options and Related Matters'. The whole project was encouraged by the Home Office and kept secret from Parliament. When the manual was in its final draft the then Home Secretary, William Whitelaw, read and sanctioned it. The preparations were carried out in complete secrecy. ACPO had produced its national manual of public order tactics for the 1980s, but it was restricted to police officers up to and including the rank of Chief Superintendent. The stage was set for one of the most significant shifts in police strategy that Britain had known.

The final stages of training in the new public order tactics were completed in 1984. They were almost perfectly on-cue for the first test of their effectiveness, which was not to suppress a riot in Hong Kong but to defeat a mass picket of striking British coal miners. ACPO relied heavily on this colonial experience in its blueprint for a control structure which both enabled and emboldened a Chief Constable to transform his force on command into a paramilitary style fighting unit. Roy Henry's Hong Kong model was imported by ACPO directly. The reality of this was captured when one senior Metropolitan officer said that policemen were being asked to behave as soldiers. He gave a graphic description of coaches leaving Hendon (police training centre in London) every Sunday for the coalfields, saying that it was like watching an embarcation for war. While the army calls them platoons, ACPO calls them Police Support Units. (4)

Monday 18 June 1984 saw the worst and final day of the violence at Orgreave. Intelligence co-ordinated by the National Reporting Centre (NRC) indicated that many striking miners would be arriving from all corners of the British coalfields. In response to this mass build-up of pickets, extra police were requested and received through the NRC. And to make sure that pickets did fall back on Orgreave, the police tightened their road-blocks in Yorkshire and on the Nottinghamshire border.

At the end of the day 93 pickets had been arrested, 79 of whom were charged with riot and unlawful assembly, and 181 PSUs, 50 police horses and 58 dogs had been deployed. (5) Orgreave had become the supreme example to date of the paramilitary approach in action.

There was a remarkable outcome to the subsequent Orgreave 'riot' trials. It was certainly a most unwelcome outcome so far as ACPO was concerned. It was the open disclosure for the first time of the existence of their new and highly contentious Public Order Manual. During the trial, under cross-examination by defence counsel, the then South Yorkshire Assistant Chief Constable, Tony Clements, agreed that, 'drumming on the shields was legitimate in the circumstances and was, indeed, authorised in the Manual'. 'What manual was this?' asked defence counsel, inviting Clements to quote the relevant section. The Assistant Chief Constable, under the direction of the trial judge, referred to a section of the Manual governing long shields, short shields and horses. ACPO's secret was out. (6) Three sections of the Manual that were read out in court caused immediate concern:

The Media, the Police & the Miners' Strike

1. The instruction to short shield officers to 'disperse and/or incapacitate demonstrators'

2. The instruction that long shield officers should give a show of force by making a formidable appearance, and

3. The stated objective of using police horses to create fear among a crowd. (7)

Following prolonged consultations with the defence, the prosecution told the judge that the Crown would not proceed with the charges. The prosecution also dropped another 79 charges against miners awaiting trial resulting from the Orgreave disturbances. The Crown's argument cited the length of time that it would take to complete outstanding files as its reasons for abandoning the prosecutions. Defence lawyers, however, maintained that this decision was taken to prevent further exposure in court of the police tactics outlined in the secret ACPO manual. The cat was out of the bag!

Orgreave on the 18 June revealed that in this country we have a standing army of highly trained police officers available to be deployed against gatherings of civilians whose congregation is disliked by politicians and senior officers - police officers whose trained tactics include the deliberate maiming and injury of persons to disperse them in complete violation of the law. (8)

Orgreave has been mythologised as the day South Yorkshire Police and the Tory government regained the control lost by the police in 1972 at Saltley Gate in Birmingham and by Ted Heath's lamentable administration in 1974. Orgreave, however, quickly entered the pageant of state repression alongside Peterloo, Tonypandy, the 1926 General Strike, attacks upon the National Unemployed Workers' Movement of the 1930s and, more recently, on the student demonstrations against austerity cuts to further and higher education and the abolition of the Education Maintenance Allowance (EMA).

Orgreave seems to have been identified by the police as the showdown with the miners, the outcome of which was to have a profound effect upon the future developments of the strike, designed to break its momentum at arguably its most critical period. Whilst the defeat of the miners at Orgreave did not end the strike, it did open the door for the use of heavier police tactics at the colliery gates afterwards.

In a wider political context, Orgreave was but an outcome of the preceding years of industrial struggle, the origins of which can be found in the emergence of a new right-wing ideology following the election of Margaret Hilda Thatcher in 1979, which would climax with the assault upon the coalfields. In this she was willingly aided and supported by a truncheon-happy police force and we saw the metamorphosis of Dixon of Dock Green's Police Constable 'Plod' into Police Constable 'Pig'!

I returned home from Orgreave later that afternoon oblivious for the moment of its significance in history but deeply shocked at what I had not only witnessed but had willingly and unapologetically participated in. I was incredulous as to the bias and selective reporting on TV later that evening concerning the battle at Orgreave. I was, however, just glad to be back safe in the bosom of those dearest to me, in the heart of a heartless world.

Notes

(1) Gerry Northam, *Shooting in the Dark*, Faber and Faber, 1988 p39

(2) Ibid.p40

(3) Ibid.p41

(4) Ibid.p52

(5) Report by Peter Wright, Chief Constable of South Yorkshire
Policing the Coal Industry Dispute in South Yorkshire 1985.

(6) Northam, op cit.p58

(7) Ibid.p58

(8) *Daily Telegraph*, 6 August, 1985

"Push Ahead On All Fronts": The Orgreave Truth and Justice Campaign
Granville Williams

> *"We have to get the feeling out there in the movement that this is the issue to back." Barbara Jackson, Secretary, OTJC.*

The Orgreave Truth and Justice Campaign Founding statement, 15 November 2012:
Seeking truth and justice for all miners victimised by the police at the Orgreave Coking Plant, South Yorkshire, June 1984.
Orgreave is part of the pattern of cover ups and lies by the police from many different forces, which are now being exposed.
We call for a full public inquiry to take place as soon as possible into the policing and subsequent statements recorded by the police at the time.
We want everyone who seeks the truth and wants justice to support us in our campaign.

THE *INSIDE OUT* PROGRAMME on Orgreave, transmitted on 22 October 2012, became the focus for a range of organisations and individuals whose concerns about police behaviour at Orgreave in June 1984 had been simmering away for years. The programme stimulated discussion on the very lively and informative email miners' information list and it led Barbara Jackson, a former member of the white collar section of the NUM, COSA, who with eight others was on strike in Sheffield in 1984-85 supporting the miners, to organise a meeting on 8 November 2012. Ten people came along to the first meeting to establish the Orgreave Truth and Justice Campaign (OTJC). Barbara Jackson says, "I had no idea at that stage what the campaign might do...I thought we might have a demonstration outside the police headquarters in Sheffield but by the end of that meeting we had ten suggestions of what we could do."

Joe Rollin was at that first OTJC meeting. Joe, a former print worker on the *Barnsley Chronicle*, moved to London and worked first at the printers Newsfax and then at West Ferry printers, at the time the biggest printing plant in Britain. "I realised there the power of the union to change people's lives – we had great wages and working conditions and at the peak printed eight or nine newspapers. I was in the GPMU (now part of UNITE) and became deputy father of the chapel. The owners changed from Lord Hollick to Richard Desmond when he took over the Express Newspaper group in 2000. Then the Barclay Brothers took over the Telegraph group from Conrad Black. The two owners fell out big time, meetings descended into farce because they couldn't get along. As always it's the workers that suffer in this situation and contracts were lost. After four years of voluntary redundancies I left and came back to Barnsley."

He now works for UNITE as a community co-ordinator at the NUM/UNITE office in Barnsley. He got involved with OTJC for a number of reasons: "I am a Barnsley lad and the strike had a massive impact on our area and still does thirty years on. I also saw the obvious links in my new role as Community Coordinator. I am very close to Sheila Coleman, who does my job as UNITE community coordinator in Liverpool. She is with the Hillsborough Justice Campaign and we have had close links with them over the last year. I also have, and always have had, a sense of what's right and wrong in the world and Orgreave was one incident within the strike that if we can get some truth and justice around that, then it will open up an inquiry into the policing of the strike and the involvement of the state in the strike."

Joe found out about the first OTJC meeting from the miners' information list. Back in May 2012 Spanish miners went on strike in defence of jobs and on 10 June the Spanish Miners' Solidarity Committee was launched to raise money and support the Spanish miners. Joe explains that people involved in the solidarity work at that time didn't use social media and so he helped with that side of things, set up a Facebook page, and was on the stall at the Durham Miners' Gala.(1) For that, and a lot of other work, he was invited to join the miners' information list.

Joe says, "I've been to numerous meetings over the years but the difference between that first OTJC meeting, and ones I normally get invited to, is that everyone took a task away from that meeting and within a week all the tasks had been done. So I realised that this group meant business and wasn't just a talking shop. The last 12 or 13 months have proved that." Joe reflected on the quality of the activists at that first meeting: "The left in this country is very good at talk, talk, but not very good at walking the walk. We had people there with a fantastic skill set who could put things into place. Within a week we launched the e-petition, we had a website and social media launched, we had connections to print T-shirts, design posters and leaflets. Really the campaign hit the ground running." (2)

The first weeks after the launch were hectic. Plans for a meeting in the New Year shifted to a meeting three weeks later on 27 November 2012. The campaign also got a massive boost on 14 November when the South Yorkshire police (SYP) self-referred to the IPCC. One of the reasons given by SYP was the revelations in Dan Johnson's programme.

However the OTJC could have sunk without trace. Then out of the blue the new campaign got big publicity from Mark Townsend at *The Observer*. Just by chance he was up in Sheffield and Barbara invited him along to the second meeting. The result was a double-page spread in *The Observer*. (3) Paul Routledge did something in the *Mirror*, Pete Lazenby in the *Morning Star* and Mark Townsend did another piece in *The Observer*. There was also very positive publicity on Radio Sheffield, BBC Look North and ITV Calendar. A visit by an American journalist, Kari Lydersen, meant that the OTJC even got coverage in the USA. (4) "The press publicity in the early days was great. We were the new kids on the block," Barbara says.

The work of building support in the trade union movement began rapidly. There was a model resolution distributed to get trade unions to support the OTJC. My union branch, Leeds NUJ, donated £200 and put a resolution forward to the annual meeting of Yorkshire and Humber TUC praising the *Inside Out* programme and urging support for the OTJC. I moved the resolution at the conference in York and quoted from a letter the OTJC had received from the branch secretary of Knottingley ASLEF, donating £100:

It has always been a great source of pride to me personally that members of this branch of ASLEF moved not one ton of coal during the year-long strike despite the best efforts of British Rail management of the time...One of our members at the meeting was at Orgreave that day and gave a harrowing account of what he saw.

Normally resolutions get passed without passionate

debate but this one enlivened the meeting with contributions from former miners now in UCATT and UNISON.

"Daily cheques from the RMT supporting us came in - they were the biggest backers initially and, through my contacts in UNITE, we put a massive press release out and were invited to speak at numerous councils and union branches," Joe remembers. The OTJC is now well connected to unions through this work and this is reflected in the steady stream of donations which come to the OTJC and the requests for speakers at meetings.

As the OTJC gained momentum people came forward with real legal experience to help – Mike McColgan, a Sheffield solicitor who was involved for the defence in the trial and acquittal of Orgreave miners in 1985; and, in February 2013, Gareth Pierce emailed very tentatively to offer her help. "That was a real high point. When she offered to help it gave us such credibility," Barbara recalls.

Paul Winter, a former Dodworth and Grimethorpe miner, is an active campaign supporter. It was an incident from the 1984-85 strike which spurred him to make a commitment:

> I was involved from the start in 1984 and came out of the pit (Dodworth) from night shift at 6 o'clock and by half past six I was on the picket line. The early part of the strike was absolutely fantastic because we were out solid and could focus on Notts. We hired coaches to go down and picket. First place we went was Whitwell where we picketed the night shift and stopped over to picket the day shift. Union men went into their canteen to speak to their workforce and they voted to come out after peaceful picketing. For the first fortnight this worked to a tee but then the government must have intervened because we had road blocks everywhere, and we couldn't move into Notts.

SETTLING SCORES:

In the early part of June, just before Orgreave, there were four of us in a car and we were flagged over and stopped as we were going to one of the pits in South Notts. We got stopped on the A1 and they asked us to turn around because we were suspected of being flying pickets. The lad driving said, "We're not picketing and it's now't to do with you where we are going. There's now't wrong with this car and if we've told you we're not picketing you cannot stop us driving down this road."

They said they'd arrest us if we didn't turn around - and they did. I spent a day in Mansfield police cell. We were told by the NUM duty solicitor to plead guilty because that many people had been arrested that it was easier to just pay the fine - £75 for obstruction. When I was stood in the dock the policeman read out his statement: "Winter said, 'You don't want us to be effective'." I was in the back of the car, I was the youngest, and I never spoke a word to anybody. I never gave it a thought again until that *Inside Out* programme came on and they were looking at Hillsborough and the fact that they were saying the same sort of set up happened at Orgreave. Eleven thousand miners were arrested during the strike – how many of them were treated like me? It was at that point I got in touch with Barbara Jackson and said, "I'm going to get involved in this campaign."

Bridget Bell was in the Potteries when the strike took off, 'one hundred per cent engaged' in the miners' support groups set up in Stoke, and then founded the North Staffs Miners' Wives Action Group which continued after the strike and was very active supporting the Justice for Mineworkers Campaign. "This is one of the threads which led me into the Orgreave campaign," she says. "In 2004 with Anne Scargill and Betty Cook we were organ-

ising an event for the 20th anniversary of the miners'
strike and Women Against Pit Closures was reformed
nationally and a year-long group of activities culminated
in a big celebration at Wortley Hall. We also had a picnic
quickly organised in about three weeks at Orgreave for
18 June and only about 12 people turned up but what
made the day for me was that Arthur Critchlow turned
up and it was an honour to meet an Orgreave veteran
who I had only seen on film."(5)

Bridget went to an OTJC meeting in Doncaster and
said she wanted to organise an Orgreave picnic for the 30th
anniversary, and that's where she has put her energies.
"There is an idea among sections of the left that organising something cultural doesn't carry the same weight as
organising a protest. I've always felt this was nonsense.
Social and cultural activity during the miners' strike ce-
mented links between women and I feel the picnic will
make a difference with the campaign." All the signs are
that it will be a fantastic 'mass picnic and festival' to be
held on 14 June at the Catcliffe Recreation Ground.

The OTJC took the decision to move meetings to different towns in the former coalfield communities to at-
tract new supporters. At the Rotherham meeting, as a
result of a piece by Phil Turner in the *Rotherham Adver-
tiser*, two former miners who were charged at Orgreave
came along. From Scotland Neil Findlay MSP contacted
OTJC about 900 Scottish miners who had come forward
about unsafe convictions and the campaign has good
links with him now.

Barbara recalls: "In the very early days we were very
fragile in terms of numbers and in terms of miners coming forward. We were taken by surprise by the pace and
speed of events but we had no structure. It took several
months to get people to take on the jobs of Treasurer
and Chair but we are there now."

The summer months of 2013 saw the OTJC make a

wider impact. "The Durham miners' gala was pretty impressive, with people clapping the banner as it came past," Joe said, "and the big TUC march in Manchester to Save the NHS with 60,000 people at it and people marching by wearing the Orgreave T-shirts."

The only setback has been the failure of the e-petition. "We honestly thought we wouldn't have any problem getting the signatures," Barbara says, "but after six months we thought we are never going to make it so we let it lie – it went to the margins." Joe thinks it was a tactical error. "We launched the petition too soon - we should have waited until now. I don't think we would have any problem now. That's the only mistake we made, the only thing we got wrong."

One big focus for the OJTC on 14 November 2013 was the demonstration with trade union banners of 60 people outside the IPCC in Wakefield to protest at the slow pace of its work. The IPCC commissioner Cindy Butts spoke to the protestors: "I apologise because I know people want answers and we are not in a position to give them those answers." She then had a meeting with a delegation inside. The event got good coverage in the regional media.

But 2014-15 is the big one, the 30th anniversary year of the epic miners' struggle. The IPCC will have to decide whether, on the basis of the evidence collected, there is the scope for an investigation into the role of SYP at Orgreave and afterwards. The 30th anniversary has triggered an amazing range of activity and events organised by the OTJC and other organisations. Joe Rollin sums it up: "We have to keep on doing what we have been doing so far. I think the picnic in June is going to be massive and there's a lot of excitement around that. We have to keep pushing at all doors, including the IPCC. The media has a place in this too, as well as our campaigning work and demonstrations. There's no one tactic that's going to crack this one for us – we have to push ahead on all fronts."

Notes

Interviews with Barbara Jackson, 21 January 2014; Joe Rollin and Bridget Bell, 22 January 2014; Paul Winter, 25 January 2014. A number of other people and organisations have played a key role in building up the work of the OTJC. I chose these four members to give an insight into the organisation's launch and activities. The OTJC can be contacted at: *orgreavejustice@hotmail.com*

(1) *https://www.facebook.com/SpanishMinersSolidarityCommittee*

(2) *https://www.facebook.com/OrgreaveTruthAndJusticeCampaign*

3) Mark Townsend, *The Observer*, 2 December, 2012, pp8-9.

4) *https://inthesetimes.com/article/14365/orgreave_coal_strike_police_brutality_1984*

(5) Yvette Vanson, *The Battle of Orgreave*, 1985. *http://www.yvettevanson.com/film/battle-orgreave*

Searching For Truth and Justice

"...the documents were never lost. They lay in un-catalogued archives, unfiled cabinets and in personal collections across numerous organisations, each with institutional interests to safeguard. They were available to, but neutralised by, the process of investigation, inquiry and scrutiny. This allowed their powerful evidence to remain hidden while myth prevailed."

Phil Scraton, 'The legacy of Hillsborough: liberating truth, challenging power' *Race & Class*, October-December 2013

SETTLING SCORES:

Reporting the Next Battle: Lessons from Orgreave
Tony Harcup

THE FIRST THAT MOST PEOPLE heard of the Battle of Orgreave was when TV newsreader Moira Stuart informed viewers of the BBC's early evening bulletin on 18 June 1984 that around 5,000 pickets at Orgreave had 'fought a pitched battle with over 2,000 police'. The screen behind her showed an enlarged still image of a T-shirted man attempting a flying kick on a police officer. That incident then formed part of the footage used to illustrate a report that the striking miners' blockade of a key South Yorkshire coking plant had seen police come under 'a barrage of stones and missiles' before 'eventually senior officers ordered in the mounted police to disperse the miners'. The post-mortem examination of how the media covered what was to prove a pivotal moment in the coal dispute began almost immediately when BBC Assistant Director General (ADG) Alan Protheroe told an internal meeting the following day that the bulletin referred to above 'might not have been wholly impartial'. (1) Three decades later that post-mortem is, in a sense, still going on.

The thirtieth anniversary of the miners' strike of

1984-85 provides an appropriate vantage point from which to examine those events because the 2014 release of Cabinet documents has confirmed what virtually any sentient being knew back in 1984: that the Thatcher government had embarked on a war of attrition against the National Union of Mineworkers as part of a plan to force the closure of at least 70 pits with the loss of more than 70,000 jobs, and to that end pressure had been applied to 'stiffen the resolve' of police. So, as others have been scrutinising those official state papers released under the 30-year-rule, I decided to use the separate Freedom of Information (FOI) Act to uncover what the BBC itself had said internally about its coverage of the strike, and specifically the events at Orgreave in the summer of 1984. It is worth noting in passing that, although the BBC comes under the FOI Act (because it is a public organisation), commercial media do not.

'A marginal imbalance'

Within weeks of the strike ending a 66-page confidential report into *The BBC's Journalism and the 1984-85 Miners' Strike* had been produced – 'for internal purposes... not for public consumption' – and its draft contents discussed at a special News and Current Affairs meeting at Broadcasting House, London, on 30 April 1985. But internal agonising – or what those of us teaching journalism within the 'hackademy' often refer to as 'reflective practice' - had begun much earlier, as can be seen in the minutes of one of the BBC's weekly News and Current Affairs meetings, dated 19 June 1984. According to the confidential minutes now released under FOI, the topic was introduced in the following way:

> ADG [Alan Protheroe] said he had found the events of the previous day very worrying; additionally, he had a feeling that the BBC's early evening coverage of Orgreave might not have been wholly impartial.

The coverage illustrated the many problems of TV coverage, not least its inability to present a "total" picture: in addition, ADG felt his often-repeated warnings against what he called "adjectival reporting" should be repeated. It was more essential than ever for the BBC's journalism to be obviously distanced from events. Peter Woon [Editor of BBC TV News] agreed that there had been a marginal imbalance in the particular bulletin, and said this was a general feeling in the newsroom. It was exceedingly difficult to edit an hour's shooting. Any departure from balance, however, was not such as to justify the NUM's view that the BBC was biased.

In the ensuing discussion, according to the minutes, issues raised included 'how neutral one could be as between law-breakers and the police', and how 'the BBC's coverage must show the extent to which the miners were to blame'. That, for many supporters of the strike, was precisely what was wrong with coverage of the previous day's events: not only did it appear to blame miners for the violence but it seemed to be the product of a mindset that *assumed* all law-breakers to be on the strikers' side of the front line.

Missing the story

Later revelations about Orgreave - and subsequent cases from Hillsborough to Plebgate - have raised doubts about 'common sense' assumptions that all police are always on the side of the angels. But this time we did not even need to wait for hindsight. Whereas BBC television's 5.40pm news bulletin on 18 June 1984 left viewers with the impression that police use of truncheons and horses had been in *response* to unprovoked violence from the miners' side, the early evening news on the rival ITN suggested it may have been the police themselves who had upped the ante. ITN's footage included mounted police charging pickets who had simply been standing around and – in a shocking scene reminiscent of the way uniformed thuggery had been unleashed on 1960s' civil rights protesters from Alabama to Derry - also showed a police officer using his truncheon to strike one man about the head, repeatedly.

According to media academic Len Masterman, who speedily dissected that day's TV coverage for his 1984 book *Television Mythologies*, in the BBC's 'eagerness to select and shape events to fit a pre-formulated interpretation, they missed by a mile what was to become the main story of Orgreave', which he argued was the issue of 'unnecessary police violence'. Worse than missing this story, he went on, was the way in which largely retaliatory actions by miners were used, 'emblematically', as visual shorthand for what the public were routinely told was 'picket line violence'. (2)

Such a critique was not the preserve of academia, as can be seen from the official account of another BBC News and Current Affairs meeting released under FOI. Minutes from 2 October 1984 record:

> ADG [Alan Protheroe] noted an extraordinary complaint from a miner alleging that the BBC had reversed sequences in a film so as to suggest that missile throwing by pickets had been followed by a police baton charge when in reality the police had moved first. John Wilson [Editor of News and Current Affairs, Radio] said it was very difficult to counter this kind of claim in a way that undid the damage of the original assertion.

Discussion then moved on to other aspects of the miners' strike and there is no evidence from the minutes that those present connected this 'extraordinary complaint' with the earlier internal acknowledgement that there had been a 'marginal imbalance' back in June of that year.

Then, towards the end of the strike, Labour MP Tony Benn used a Commons debate on the dispute to accuse the BBC of *deliberate* bias:

The mass media gathered up there in the press gallery have been pouring out propaganda against the miners. For example, when BBC television covered the Orgreave picket, it showed stones being thrown, and then cavalry charges being made by the police. I know from BBC editors who took part in that bulletin that there were three cavalry charges by the police before a single stone was thrown. But the BBC, pretending to be impartial, put out a bulletin designed to mislead the British people about the sources of violence. (3)

Despite the seriousness of Benn's accusation it was not addressed directly in *The BBC's Journalism and the 1984-85 Miners' Strike*, produced by Alan Protheroe and his special assistant Roy Roberts for internal BBC consumption in May 1985. This is as near as it came:

The violence at the Orgreave coking works at this time provided some of the most dramatic and enduring images of the dispute, and again illustrated the difficulty of television cameramen in any situation in securing a *total* picture, particularly when their freedom to operate is constrained. It is a difficulty that has been encountered before in the Middle East or in Northern Ireland, but never before in mainland Britain. At such times it is particularly important for those telling the story that accompanies the pictures to avoid the pitfalls and dangers of adjectival reporting, and to distance themselves appropriately from events. A topic of concern at this time arising out of incidents such as Orgreave was whether the BBC was attempting to adopt a posture of neutrality between those who broke the law and those who sought to maintain law and order. It seemed, however, appropriate to do so at a time when police tactics were of considerable concern in a substantial section of the community.

Protheroe's document did take a reflective and at times self-critical look at how the BBC reported a dispute that 'has received more coverage than any other in the history of British broadcasting', but it also contained more than a hint of *if both sides complain of bias then we must be doing OK.*

It was left to former BBC man Alastair Hetherington (then a media professor at the University of Stirling) to defend the specifics of the BBC's 18 June bulletin, explaining in an article six months after the strike ended: 'The testimony of every reporter to whom I have talked is the same. The police did not start the violence at Orgreave that day. Why the BBC has made no response to the allegations that it reversed the order of events is unclear.' (4) Hetherington found that the single most shocking incident of police violence captured by ITN - of an officer beating a miner repeatedly with a truncheon - had been missed by the BBC's crew because of a fault with a camera which meant it filmed only in seven second bursts. ITN had extra cameras there that day, he added. Indeed, the minutes of the News and Current Affairs meeting of 30 April 1985 noted that, at the time of the strike, ITN had three cameras in the field for every BBC one.

'No truth whatsoever'

The strike ended, pit after pit closed, but the Orgreave story never quite went away, and in 1991 the National Union of Mineworkers' journal *The Miner* reported that the BBC had finally admitted screening its footage in the wrong order in error. Replying to a member of the Concerned Citizens of Cambridge group who had apparently been prompted to write to the BBC after hearing Tony Benn repeat his allegation of deliberate bias,

Martin Hart (on behalf of then BBC Director General Michael Checkland) wrote that on 18 June 1984 there had been 'a mistake made in the haste of putting the news together. The end result was that an editor inadvertently reversed the occurrence of the actions of the police and of the pickets'. Hart added that there was 'no truth whatsoever' in the claim that this had been deliberate. (5)

That was more or less it until 2007 when, after the BBC announced an inquiry into some documentary footage of the Queen apparently being screened out of sequence in a misleading way, Simon Pirani (former editor of *The Miner*) wrote to Director General Mark Thompson to suggest the Orgreave incident be added to the investigation. Thompson refused, arguing that it would serve no useful purpose. (6)

Now the thirtieth anniversary has prompted renewed interest in the strike, and the release of Cabinet documents, combined with material obtained from the BBC and revealed in this chapter, may contribute to a greater public understanding of the events of 1984-85 and how they were reported. Oddly, however, we have no further details of precisely what prompted the BBC's 1991 Orgreave admission because, as I was informed by the BBC's Senior Compliance Manager for FOI: 'We do not hold any correspondence regarding the complaint you refer to by a member of the public; information regarding public correspondence is routinely destroyed in accordance with the BBC's Corporate Retention Schedule.'

Thirty years on, does any of this matter? After all, the mining communities were not defeated as a result of one TV news bulletin, and the totality of BBC coverage also included more in-depth analysis on *Newsnight* and *Panorama,* some genuine grassroots local radio reporting from pit villages and soup kitchens, and national radio listeners had the benefit of reports by labour correspondent, Nicholas Jones. Jones was singled out in *The BBC's*

Journalism and the 1984-85 Miners' Strike for his 'tireless, authoritative, and perceptive contribution', demonstrating 'a grip on the central and sensitive aspects of the story that was second to none'. Also, albeit six months after the battle itself, the BBC even broadcast an edition of the access programme *Open Space* presented by Sheffield Policewatch, prompting Protheroe to tell the 30 April 1985 News and Current Affairs meeting that he had been 'haunted' by the contrast between the group's material on Orgreave and the BBC's own. Those present explained this discrepancy by reference to the risk of anti-media violence from pickets (of which there was undoubtedly some), insufficient resources, and 'the tendency of the police to behave well when cameras were present'.

Beyond the Beeb, ITN and *Channel 4 News* also provided broadcast reportage, with the latter often praised by strike supporters for its balance of coverage. And journalists on alternative media went out of their way to report from the miners' side of the picket lines. (7) But as a rule of thumb, the more alternative and grassroots the reporting, the more likely it was to be confined to the margins with relatively small audiences. For millions of people the BBC's teatime news *was* the news. So, when TV's 'impartial' news reporting seemed to provide powerful visual evidence for the unashamed anti-strike propaganda filling many Fleet Street newspapers, the combined impact on public opinion ought not to be discounted.

Lessons for the future

Clearly today's media landscape is very different with 24-hour broadcasting, multiple channels, the internet and catch-up services all eroding the importance of the sort of 'appointment viewing' represented by BBC TV News in 1984. Arguably an even bigger change has been the emergence of social media and the ability of ordinary people armed with mobile phones to record and report events for themselves. Three decades ago the UK mainstream media got away with largely ignoring John Harris's powerful photograph of a mounted policeman swinging a truncheon at Lesley Boulton at Orgreave, but could such a media shut-out succeed in these days of Twitter, user-generated content and so-called 'citizen journalism'? (8)

Before we comfort ourselves too much with the thought that it could not, it is worth recalling that the inaccurate police account of how newspaper-seller Ian Tomlinson died during the G20 protests in London in 2009 was at first swallowed whole by the bulk of the media. True, a different picture then emerged, but only because one journalist adopted the good reporter's default position of scepticism and followed his 'hunch' that there might 'be more to the story'. The key amateur footage that disproved the police line was sent to *Guardian* journalist Paul Lewis largely because he had already shown himself willing to combine the latest online communication technologies with traditional reporting methods (including face-to-face meetings and visiting the scene) to question the police version of events. (9)

In other words, the presence of multiple camera phones will not on its own alter the balance of media power, and reporters armed with good old-fashioned scepticism can still play a vital role when it comes to informing the public. Journalists contemplating how to report the next Orgreave or the next G20 could learn much from looking back at how both events were covered at the time and at what subsequently emerged to contradict the official narrative. They might conclude that, perhaps even more significant than the way the events of 18 June 1984 were reported on the day itself, was the way that for a whole year the very language of news was so often turned against communities that were resisting the harsh economics of Thatcher's Britain. When workplaces could be declared 'uneconomic' by the stroke of a pen, when a strike that was essentially *for* 'the right to work' could be portrayed as an *attack on* the 'right to work', and when the daily headlines could focus on a minority ending the strike rather than the majority remaining out, surely something had gone wrong with the language and values of news. Or perhaps journalists' usual news values were simply not up to the job of reporting such a multi-faceted story.

104   There are clues to all this to be found within the BBC's own post-mortem report, *The BBC's Journalism and the 1984-85 Miners' Strike*, for those who look closely enough. 'Inevitably, news coverage concentrated on the changing elements of the story, rather than those that did not change,' notes Protheroe at one point. But was that really inevitable? Elsewhere, he refers to television showing 'the real nature of picketing'. But did it really? The more normal routine of small and peaceful picketing was rarely covered or even acknowledged, squeezed out by what one local radio news editor called 'the apparent television hunger for violence on the picket line at the expense of greater understanding'. Another local radio station even adopted a policy of only covering pickets on its patch if there were more than 500 pickets present; so much for reflecting the 'real nature' of most picket lines, which were often mundane and even good-humoured.

And finally, there is one point that really ought to be taken to heart, not just by journalists but by those who set editorial policies and budgets. It is the comment from journalists and production staff who covered the strike for *Newsnight* and *Panorama*, who are quoted in the report as pointing out that, when it came to gaining people's trust and getting below the surface of a story, 'no substitute existed for the making and fostering of direct face-to-face contacts'. That remains the case even in the age of Twitter. But, as the Ian Tomlinson story demonstrates, a healthy dose of scepticism is also required.

Notes

(1) This quote and the BBC quotes that follow come from confidential documents released under FOI in December 2013.

(2) *Television Mythologies* by Len Masterman (Comedia, 1984), pp99-109.

(3) Tony Benn speech 4 February 1985, *http://hansard.millbanksystems. com/commons/1985/feb/04/coal-industry-dispute- 1#S6CV0072P0_19850204_HOC_295*

(4) 'The empire that won't strike back', *Guardian*, 2 September 1985.

(5) 'We reversed Orgreave pictures', *The Miner*, October 1991.

(6) Thanks to Simon Pirani for details of this correspondence, which was previously published on www.simonpirani.com

(7) See *Alternative Journalism, Alternative Voices* by Tony Harcup (Routledge, 2013), pp81-98.

(8) See 'The making of an icon' by Michael Bailey and Julian Petley in *Shafted*, edited by Granville Williams (CPBF, 2009), pp91-99.

(9) See 'How "citizen journalism" aided two major *Guardian* scoops' by Paul Lewis, *http://onlinejournalismblog.com/2011/11/01/paul-lewis- how-citizen-journalism-aided-two-major-guardian-scoops-guest-post/*

From Orgreave to Wapping:
The Real Enemy Within
John Bailey

THOSE WHOSE FORMATIVE YEARS were just after the Second World War will remember the widely promoted view that Britain had the best of everything, including the best police force in the world whose constables and officers were citizens in uniform; the best form of justice, and a monarchy to match. But that was long, long ago.

Now we are so far from that fiction that Britain's police forces are, it seems, more centred on keeping public order than catching the new breed of criminal represented by those running big international corporations, including publishers and bankers, who feel they are well above the law and are able to use the state's police force to enforce their new-found positions of power.

This development is important because the British way of policing has informed the police forces of many countries where the empire once exerted influence, particularly when using force to maintain public order, as governments regard it, is concerned.

Today most people not associated with criminal intent will have met the police on the streets only when making their voices heard in protest or demonstration.

In everyday circumstances it is extremely difficult to find a single policeman anywhere near a street unless it's in a patrol car. Where such huge numbers of so-called riot police come from at times of protest is a mystery. Are they waiting somewhere fully equipped with all the necessary tools of aggressive enforcement? The answer must be that they are because the reaction to protest and demonstration by the police in Britain is now time-honoured by its speed and aggressive intervention. However, this confrontational approach to public order is not new in Britain; it was established before the formation of a state police force in 1829 that is now easily identified as the Metropolitan Police Force – the Met.

For example, the assembly at Spa Fields in central London on Monday 13 May 1833 is a good example of how the Met, formed just four years previously, dealt with peaceful protest. The committee of the National Union of the Working Classes was about to address a meeting of between one and two thousand people when the police descended unannounced on the crowd from nearby stables where they had been hiding. At the time the *Gentleman's Magazine* reported: 'The police having completely surrounded the actors and spectators of the scene commenced a general and indiscriminate attack on the populace inflicting broken heads alike on those who stood and parleyed and those who endeavoured to retreat'. *New Bell's Weekly Messenger* added: 'The police came on and used their staves pretty freely . . . many heads were broken'. These reports will sound familiar to those who have tried to protest in recent times, but today a report of such police action in breaking up a demonstration is unlikely to appear in print and to be carefully distorted if shown on national television in order to show the police reacting to intimidation rather than orchestrating such violence.

Clearly the scene was set all those years ago when it came to dealing with the mob *(mobile vulgus)* as any group of protestors were commonly known, and that sums up the state's continuing view of those not prepared to accept the political status quo.

If non-violent demonstrators are restrained but refuse to back down then recent events show clearly that they will be physically attacked and struck down as the police, acting as agents of the state, enforce its laws. Tactics designed to make demonstrations irrelevant by limiting them to specific areas separate from the object of their discontent, from the public and in some cases from the media, make them more easily ignored. And the regulation that makes demonstrations without advance police permission illegal has further constrained the actions of those prepared to voice their discontent.

As anyone who is involved in challenging anything from industrial disputes to government policy that includes going to war, to local issues that demand a public voice to be heard knows, there is a sense that it is protestors versus the state in the form of its police force and further, according to the media, the state is always right. Actions by the police in controlling the public, the very people who pay for Britain's 43 police forces, has led to a situation where demonstrations are regarded as threats to the state to be contained and attacked with all force both necessary and unnecessary. And nowhere was that more evident than in the famous industrial disputes in the latter years of the twentieth century.

That period was important because of the heightened political involvement in policing that has now become the norm. Anti-union laws in force from the early eighties gave police extended powers to limit protests and support for those involved in legitimate industrial action. Picketing was severely limited as was action by other workers in support of strikers. The action of police in enforcing the removal of these traditional rights of protest and support led to many violent confrontations not previously witnessed and were never more apparent than during the miners' strike in 1984 and those in dispute with Murdoch at Wapping in 1986.

These two disputes showed clearly where politics and industrial relations overlapped. At a time when printers gave overwhelming support to miners throughout British coalfields in every way possible, the British press, the state and its police forces were doing all they could to portray striking miners as criminals. This resulted in the criminalisation of innocent miners by hundreds of policemen who falsified their reports of incidences in order to secure convictions at court hearings. The source of the authority for such actions can only be guessed at; it is difficult to imagine that it was a local, spontaneous action by so many individuals with their own agendas.

Printers who were asked to produce newspapers that viciously and untruthfully portrayed miners as mindless aggressors trying to promote civil unrest refused to print incriminating articles that did not offer those vilified an equally prominent Right of Reply.

This was a radical form of protest not previously exercised in Britain, inspired by the Campaign for Press and Broadcasting Freedom, who promoted the Right of Reply that gained acceptance by all the printing unions and the National Union of Journalists. Throughout Fleet Street printers refused to allow crude, distorted views of strikers to be printed and many newspapers contained blank pages or, in some instances, editions did not appear at all because printers pressed for a right of reply that was not forthcoming. In all seriousness and without a trace of irony, editors and proprietors complained that this was interference with their freedom of the press to print whatever distortions suited their political agendas, a self-appointed right that had been exercised for more than a century and underpinned a false idea that Britain enjoyed a free press.

To some extent the printers' actions limited the supply of biased propaganda that normally reached readers and handed workers a new tool with which to combat the overwhelming influence of a corrupt press. These actions made many printers feel closer to those they had already supported by sending lorry-loads of food and clothes to coalfields and by inviting families into their homes. More importantly workers were able to express their solidarity with those in struggle by thwarting the draconian new anti-union laws. This solidarity was to be an important factor when printers were subjected to violence and intimidation by a police force in total collaboration with Rupert Murdoch's News International Wapping printing plant and the state's union-busting, politically inspired laws during the last big industrial dispute in Britain during 1986-87.

In 2011 at a meeting that focused on the policing of protests and demonstrations, Charlotte Gerada, then General Secretary of LSE's Student Union, commented on the police violence prevalent at protests. She said that being kettled for six and a half hours can cause a pacifist such as herself to want to 'smash things up'. She also said that it was important to explore how the media portrayed such violence. She encouraged people to think about the meaning of the violence and whether the press described those who initiated it accurately.

The increasing fallout in terms of mistrust of the police across so many incidents including Hillsborough, Orgreave, deaths in custody and false evidence by police officers in court proceedings now comes as no surprise to miners and printers and those involved in recent demonstrations and protests.

The attitude and violent reaction of the police were common factors in both the miners' and the printers' disputes. At Wapping all the aggressive tactics practised on miners were apparent, including charging demonstrators on horseback and gross acts of intimidation. As the primary purpose of police in 1984 was to allow coal into power stations and to give every opportunity for strike breakers to get into work without challenge, so the primary duty of police at Wapping was to ensure Murdoch's lorries left his plant without hindrance, even without allowing the six legitimate pickets at the factory gate to inform anyone going in or out of the printworks about the nature of and the reasons for the strike.

The resolution of the miners was more than a match for the initial, local police opposition they faced in persecuting their grievances but, as at Wapping, the involvement of other forces, particularly the Met, meant there was less accountability to those that the local constabulary were meant to protect and consequently less concern about the damage, both physical and mental, visited upon the whole populations of mining villages by these rank outsiders. This was less of a problem at Wapping because the printers already knew the bad reputation of the Met from previous experiences such as the Grunwick protests as early as 1977, and how hard it would be even to maintain the minimal rights they had as strikers. And how right they were.

Of the 6000 sacked by Murdoch, many were women who had served Murdoch and helped make his fortune just as had the printers, but the police saw only those who offered some obstruction to their overriding intention to allow Murdoch's papers to be distributed from his printworks. As a consequence many women and their children, who had paraded peacefully in protest to Murdoch's plant, were repeatedly charged by police horses and suffered from the same aggressive truncheon blows as their male working colleagues.

This was never more apparent than during events on 24 January 1987 when one of the largest demonstrations numbering as many as 25,000 supporters joined a printers' march through London to Murdoch's plant at Wapping. Events of that evening were monitored by the Haldane Society of Socialist Lawyers whose report of the actions of the Met will come as no surprise to miners who suffered similarly in 1984 and to those who have read the reports on policing at Orgreave now made public 30 years too late.

The Haldane report *A Case to Answer?* begins by calling for a public enquiry into police tactics and behaviour on that evening, a call that was echoed by MPs including Tony Benn, and Ron Leighton, a SOGAT member and one-time printer and union official at *The Sun*, that were ignored by the government and whose questions about police behaviour on that occasion were met with complete disingenuity.

The Haldane report notes that the huge crowd eventually was densely packed into a small area opposite the printworks that was cordoned off, as were many streets, by police in riot gear. This greatly heightened the tension and led to panic as police began charging into demonstrators with no intention other than to frighten and intimidate. Subsequent charges by baton-wielding riot police caused further panic because police cordons meant that there was no way the crowd could disperse, just as at Spa fields in 1833. These attacks on peaceful protesters provoked a reaction, something the police were clearly expecting, that in turn prompted an attack on horseback by riders using long batons and truncheons to batter men, women and children around the head and shoulders.

Blindingly bright spotlights presaged continued charges by riot police at 45 minute intervals by which time the crowd had thinned considerably and those remaining had moved into a fenced-in square. This led to further aggressive charges directly into the middle of the protestors with no result except further injuries administered by truncheon blows delivered at random. Further panic ensued among the largely peaceful crowd that was borne out by the fact that only 67 arrests were made by police snatch squads from a crowd estimated to be over 25,000.

All this aggressive behaviour and intimidatory violence by the police was in direct contravention to the guidelines of the Association of Chief Police Officers (ACPO) that were issued in the wake of disturbances in Bristol, Brixton and Toxteth in 1981.

The Haldane report states from the guidelines directly about the use of truncheons: "Truncheons are supplied to police officers to protect themselves if violently attacked . . . and to be used in extreme cases when all other attempts to arrest have failed. Truncheon blows, where necessary, should be aimed at the arms, legs and torso rather than at the head as these parts are least likely to suffer serious injury." Blair Peach, a teacher who was demonstrating in London in 1979, was killed by truncheon blows to the head by special patrol group police officers who were involved in breaking up a protest in a similar manner to that which took place at Wapping.

As at Orgreave and other places during the miners' strike, these guidelines were wilfully disregarded that evening at Wapping. There were 19 head injuries attributable to truncheoning treated at one first-aid post nearby and others were treated in local hospitals; one protestor was treated for a fractured skull.

The Haldane legal observers also noted that riot police in fireproof overalls and NATO-style crash helmets could not be identified because their overalls bore no numbers and that some constables who normally would be identifiable had deliberately obscured their numbers by covering them or unfastening their epaulettes. In response to complaints the Home Office stated blandly that it was an offence for police officers not to display their identification numbers on their uniforms.

The same casual dismissal accompanied evidence that

the Met had used a chemical spray on demonstrators snatched by squads of police officers later in the evening as they made their way home or were drinking in nearby pubs that were ruthlessly raided, ransacked and arrests made.

The similarities with Orgreave were even more apparent when it came to mounted police charging into crowds of protestors at speed. Again ACPO guidelines were ignored. These state: "A warning to the crowd should always be given before adopting mounted dispersal tactics", but no warning was given and there was nowhere for the majority of the crowd to go. Clearly this was once again intimidation, the purpose being to stop strikers and their families from coming to further demonstrations. ACPO guidelines state that mounted officers should have halted before reaching the demonstrators, not charging through them, and the use by mounted police of their three-foot truncheons was also unlawful. Of course all this was denied in parliament but photographs show exactly that this happened during charges and that mounted officers used long truncheons and anything else that came to hand.

The best that could be said of such police action on that and on other occasions during recent strikes and demonstrations is that the police lost control of their thuggish officers, and to protect their wrongdoing on this and other occasions the direct assault on journalists and photographers was a deliberate provocation that must never be forgotten or forgiven. There is extensive evidence of how the police singled out photographers and camera crews at the scene; at least eleven received hospital treatment, two for serious injuries. Even so, many give vital verbal as well as photographic accounts of some horrific behaviour of the police rioting at Wapping that night.

To increase tension and intimidation, the mayor of London is calling for water cannons to be used against protestors and demonstrators. Those who have experienced the aggression of police officers as part of a military exercise against demonstrators at Orgeave, Wapping and elsewhere in Britain, can deliver a clear message to the mayor: they know already who the real the enemy within is.

The Shadow of the Strike: *Brassed Off*
Julian Petley

GIVEN THAT THE 1984-85 COAL dispute was one of the key events to have taken place in Britain in the second half of the twentieth century, it might seem extraordinary that it is represented in only one British feature film, and even then somewhat peripherally. This was *Billy Elliot* (Stephen Daldry, 2000). But although this was developed by Channel 4 and the independent British company Redwing Films, it was funded by Fox Searchlight, and this seriously limited the extent to which the film could raise overtly political issues. As the writer of *The Full Monty* (Peter Cattaneo, 1997), Simon Beaufoy, stated: 'It seems that political messages have to be so hidden in films these days that they are almost invisible'. (1)

Paradoxically, it was left to a film set nearly ten years after the strike to raise these issues, even if only sporadically, in a direct, head-on manner. This was *Brassed Off* (Mark Herman, 1996) which, being funded largely by Channel 4 itself, managed to avoid the pitfalls commonly associated with American-financed British films aimed fairly and squarely at the international, and particularly US, market. As Mike Wayne has argued: 'Because of its conditions of production, it has a primary mode of address to a UK national audience and this opens up a space for a great deal more attention to the specificities of political conflict and social inequality' than do films such as *Billy Elliot* and *The Full Monty*. (2)

Brassed Off is set in the small Yorkshire mining community of Grimley in 1992. The pit, though highly profitable, is threatened with closure by the British Coal Corporation, which has offered the miners a tempting financial package if they vote to accept redundancy in a forthcoming ballot, a package which will be withdrawn if they vote to reject the offer. Meanwhile, its spirits sinking and buoyed up only by its conductor Danny (Pete Postlethwaite), the colliery brass band prepares for a national competition. Several of the band members want to throw in the towel but are dissuaded from doing so out of loyalty to, and a certain fear of, Danny, whose lungs are clearly beginning to pack up as a result of his life down the pit.

Grimley is clearly based on Grimethorpe, where some of the film was actually shot and which possesses the world-famous brass band that provides the film with its soundtrack. In its heyday, Grimethorpe colliery was known as the 'golden pulley pit' because it was one of the most productive coal mines in Britain, producing more than a million tons of coal annually. The colliery and its related industries employed over 6000 workers. These included the South Side coal preparation plant and a £20 million pressurised fluidised bed-test facility, the biggest in the world, to efficiently burn coal in a way to protect the environment. The colliery was closed in 1993 by the British Coal Corporation, the name given to the erstwhile National Coal Board in 1987 by a Tory government driven by bitter ideological hostility to the very idea of nationalised industries. Explosive experts razed the fluidised-bed plant's combustion tower to the ground in January 1994. British Coal said they were axing the world-beating Grimethorpe project because of lack of government backing.

In 1985, in the wake of the strike, 25 pits were closed down, including Cortonwood, where the strike actually began. Between then and 1992, another 97 pits were axed, and when that year Michael Heseltine became President of the Board of Trade, he announced that 31 out of the remaining 50 deep mines would be closed, with a loss of 31,000 jobs. Grimethorpe was one of the victims of this programme of closures. Levels of unemployment, crime and drug abuse soared there, as they did in other former pit villages. Before the closure, crime in Grimethorpe was 30% below the national average; afterwards it was 20% above it. In 1994, an EU study of deprivation named Grimethorpe as the poorest village in the UK and, indeed, as amongst the poorest in Europe. This at least had the virtue of making the village eligible for European structural funds, and these helped to kick-start a slow process of regeneration which has continued to this day, although how the present government's savage cutbacks to public funding in the name of 'austerity' will affect Grimethorpe and the many other villages like it remains very much to be seen.

When the film was originally released, its poster promoted it as 'a comedy that hits all the right notes' and featured a quote from the *Mirror*, which called it 'the most enjoyable feel-good British movie since *Four Weddings and a Funeral*'. Such a comparison seems quite bizarrely wide of the mark, but what some have regarded as its feel-good elements have frequently led to comparisons with *Billy Elliot*. These at least put it in the right class bracket, but as one of the film's reviewers on the Internet Movie Database (IMDb) exclaimed: 'How anyone can call it a comedy is beyond me'. And the least comic and most political elements of the film are precisely those which relate back to the 1984-85 strike.

SETTLING SCORES:

Foremost amongst these are the long-term scars left on the community and its inhabitants by the strike. These manifest themselves in various ways. For example, in the fact that the one thing calculated to end in physical violence in Grimley is to call someone a scab. They are also there in the utter weariness of the workforce, which leads them in the end to accept the redundancy offer by a vote of four to one, in the conviction, based on ten years of experience of Thatcherite management, that the pit will ultimately be closed whether or not it is profitable. This conviction turns out to be entirely well-founded when it is revealed that the management had decided on closure two years before commissioning a report on the mine's future, which shows that it is economically viable but which they don't even bother to read once it is delivered. The scars are also clearly visible in the very evident suspicion of the rank and file miners that their union representatives are not doing their utmost to protect their members' long-term employment prospects during the redundancy negotiations. Significantly these scenes were cut out – presumably as too 'boring' – when the film was released in America, where its distributors, Miramax, described it thus:

> This delightfully entertaining comedy treat features lovable stars Ewan McGregor *(I Love You Phillip Morris)* and Tara Fitzgerald *(Sirens)* as two old friends – and ex-lovers – whose surprise reunion turns their lives, and the lives of everyone else in a small mining town, hilariously upside down. Also starring screen favorite Pete Postlethwaite *(The Town)*, don't miss all the fun to be had in *Brassed Off*.

This absolute twaddle is reproduced on Amazon. com, leading one reviewer to comment that: 'This marketing copy should win an award for completely missing the point'. Similarly, a reviewer on the Internet Movie Database (IMDb) noted that: 'Having just purchased the

DVD, I found the brief write-up on the box to be way off the mark. It touts this film as some kind of romantic and hilarious comedy, never once even gazing past the real subject matter of the film'.

The shadow of the strike also looms large in the distant relationship between Rita (Lill Roughley), an active member of the Women Against Pit Closure group camped at the gates of the colliery, and her euphonium-playing husband Harry (Jim Carter), summed up in her remark that 'ten years ago before the strike, you were full of fight, packed full of passion; now you just do nowt, just blow your bloody trumpet', to which he replies, sadly: 'At least people listen to us'. But above all the strike lives on in the figure of Phil (Stephen Tompkinson), Danny's son, who is still in serious debt as a result of being not only on strike but also in prison and suspended from his job for over a year after the strike ended, both on account of his union activism. As a result, his house is being gradually stripped by the loan sharks to whom he owes £12,000.

Phil also has an alter ego, the particularly grotesque clown Mr Chuckles, a role which he plays at children's parties in order to try to pay off his debts. In these scenes we glimpse an affluent middle-class lifestyle totally at odds with that of the miners, which makes Phil's eruptions of rage in these sedate settings all the more striking. In one of these, as he is being hurriedly paid off by an embarrassed mother after one of his conjuring tricks has gone disastrously wrong, his parting words are: 'I'm a miner. You remember them love? Dinosaurs, dodos, miners'. But his real tour-de-force occurs at, of all things, a harvest festival, at which he regales the assembled children with the following parable:

> So God was creating man, and his little assistant
> came up to him and said: 'Hey, we've got all of these
> bodies left, but we're right out of brains, we're right

out of hearts, and we're right out of vocal chords'.
And God said: 'Fuck it. Sow 'em up anyway, smack
smiles on their faces and make 'em talk out their
arses'. And lo, God created the Tory Party.

Being told that he should be ashamed of behaving
like this in the house of God serves only to provoke a
further diatribe: 'He can take John Lennon, he can take
those three young lads down at Ainsley colliery, he's
even thinking of taking my old man, and Margaret
bloody Thatcher lives. So what's he sodding playing at,
eh?' (3) By contrast, the only mention of Thatcher in
Billy Elliot, which is, after all, set during the strike itself, is
when we hear a voice on the radio referring to her desig-
nation of the striking miners as the 'enemy within'. In
Brassed Off the indescribably bizarre scene of Phil's attempted suicide, in which, dressed as Mr Chuckles, he
attempts to hang himself from a crane, the whole agony
of despair caused by the strike and its aftermath is
summed up in a singularly indelible image.

Direct political discourse is also at the heart of Danny's
speech at the Albert Hall after the band has won the finals
of the national band championship:

The band behind me will tell you that this trophy
means more to me than owt else in the whole world.
But they'd be wrong. The truth is, I thought it
mattered. I thought that music mattered, but does it
bollocks. Not compared to how people matter. Us
winning this trophy won't mean bugger all to most
people, but us refusing it, like we're going to do now,
well, then it becomes news. [Sure enough, the press
photographers suddenly take an interest and start
snapping away]. That way I'll not be talking to myself,
will I? Because over the last ten years this bloody
government has systematically destroyed an entire
industry, and not just our industry, our communities,
our homes, our lives, all in the name of progress, and

for a few lousy bucks. And I'll tell you something else you might not know. Well, a fortnight ago this band's pit was closed, and another 100 men lost their jobs. And that's not all they lost. Most of them lost the will to win a while ago. A few of them lost the will to fight. But when it comes to losing the will to live, to breathe, the point is that if this lot were seals or whales you'd all be up in bloody arms. But they're not, are they? No, they're not, they're just ordinary, common or garden, decent human beings. Not one of them with an ounce of bloody hope left. Oh aye, they can knock out a bloody good tune, but what the fuck does that matter?

Equally political, albeit in the broad sense of the word, is the film's final scene, in which the band, playing Elgar's Pomp and Circumstance March No.1 on the open top of a double decker bus, passes the Houses of Parliament. 'Land of hope and bloody glory' murmurs Danny, and a subtitle puts the struggle shown in the film firmly in its wider context: 'Since 1984 there have been 140 pit closures in Britain at the cost of nearly a quarter of a million jobs'. It is difficult to regard this scene as anything other than a bitter, even if somewhat oblique, condemnation of a government which deliberately destroyed an entire industry, and indeed of a political system which made such a thing possible. It is thus particularly gratifying to note that the political message of this film – missold as it was both in Britain and the US – is abundantly clear to many of the reviewers on the IMDb and on Amazon's British and American sites. Take, for example, this comment on the IMDb from a writer who is clearly American:

> I applaud the political message. I grew up near an
> industrial town; one centered on the auto industry,
> heavy machinery, and agri-business. As I got older, I
> watched it disintegrate, through the 70s and 80s, as

the grain embargo, auto industry woes and recession bled the life out of the town. It has never recovered. Many of us felt that Reagan and Thatcher, and their descendants, were monsters who sold their people out for a quick buck; while the parties that were supposed to represent the workers and middle class joined in the takings. To us, this isn't an anti-Thatcher film; it's the truth.

Danny's Albert Hall speech is surely aimed as much at the audience watching the film as at the audience in the Albert Hall, if not more so, since the latter is made up of supporters of brass bands such as Grimley's, who can also be expected to have experienced the effects of the onslaught of Thatcherism on the working class. And it is all the more powerful for being delivered by Danny, whose incarnation by Pete Postlethwaite is so intense that it quite eclipses the film's more light-hearted elements. The fact that Danny knows that he is dying does not diminish his determination – blazing forth from his eyes in every shot – that the band will win the contest; indeed it only increases it. Because, in the end, music *does* matter in this context. The struggle to keep the pit open may have been lost, the Tories may have effectively destroyed the British coal industry, and a much wider defeat may have been inflicted not only on the working class but on all working people in Britain, but, as Danny says to the band in an earlier scene:

The trouble with you lot is that you've got no pride. And you know one thing more than owt else round here that symbolises pride is this bloody band, that's what. Ask anybody. If they close down the pit, knock it down, fill it up, like they've done with all bloody rest, no trace in years to come, then there'll be only one reminder of a hundred years of hard graft – this bloody band. They can shut up the unions, they can shut up the workers, but I'll tell you one thing for nothing – they'll never shut us up. We'll play on loud as ever.

This is not for a moment to argue that music, or indeed culture in general, matters more than, or as much as, employment and working people's rights, but it is to insist on the importance of memory and representation to historical struggle. In many former mining areas, the very last traces of the pits have been utterly, and no doubt deliberately, erased from the face of the earth ('the pithead baths is a supermarket now', in the words of Max Boyce), and it is thus vital that the memory of the 1984-85 strike and of its aftermath is kept alive wherever and by whatever means possible – not simply in mining museums but in films such as *Brassed Off*, in television programmes like *The Battle of Orgreave* (Channel 4, 2001), on the Internet, and, of course, in books such as this. This battle for memory is made all the more essential by the fact that, at the time of its occurrence, the strike was so viciously misrepresented by the mainstream media – with the honourable exception of Channel 4 which, among its many other contributions to putting the historical record straight, produced this remarkable film.

Notes

(1) Simon Beaufoy (1998), 'Hidden agendas', *Sight and Sound*, March, p.61.

(2) Mike Wayne (2006), 'The performing northern working class in British cinema: cultural representation and its political economy', *Quarterly Review of Film and Video*, 23: 4, pp.287-97.

(3) No such pit as Ainsley exists. However, in the course of coal-picking during the strike, two boys were killed by a slag heap collapsing at Goldthorpe, South Yorkshire and another boy was killed by a similar collapse at Sharlston, West Yorkshire.

Granville Williams

IT'S BEEN CLEANED OFF THE BRIDGE now, but for a year or
two as I drove towards Ackworth from Upton, a former
mining village where I live in West Yorkshire, I could
read a scrawled message on it – 'Superdrug Abuses'.

In 2009, on the 25th anniversary of the miners' strike, I
got an insight into why an angry, frustrated person would
put that protest message on the bridge. I also witnessed
how a combination of trade union solidarity, community
support and the determination of workers not to be
squashed by a multinational company can win through
against all the odds in the depth of a grim recession.

Local newspapers, ideally, should give us the information about what's going on in our communities. A front
page spread in my local weekly paper, the *Hemsworth and
South Elmsall Express* on 2 July 2009 had the headline 'Cash
from our pockets: Workers' fury at firm's cost-cutting
plans' and detailed the way the company planned a series of
cost-cutting measures at the Superdrug depot on the Dale
End warehousing site near South Elmsall. The 5 November
issue carried the announcement of an indefinite strike, 'All
out at Superdrug' after the workforce set up a 24-hour picket starting from 5.30 am Wednesday 4 November. (1)

South Elmsall used to have a pit – Frickley Colliery – which sustained the local economy. Frickley was renowned for its militancy and proudly boasted it was 'second to none'. Only four of the 1,800 men scabbed during the year-long strike – the explanation was 'they were outsiders'. In 1987, when Arthur Scargill stood for re-election as NUM President, the atmosphere and enthusiastic support for him, when he spoke in the Pretoria Working Men's Club, South Elmsall, was palpable. You would have been hard-pressed to believe that the miners had returned to work defeated in March 1985.

Indeed, when the men marched back with their families and supporters on 5 March 1985, Kent miners, in a desperate, last-ditch effort, picketed Frickley Colliery. The miners turned back - even after twelve hard months the principle that you do not cross picket lines still stood.

When Frickley closed in November 1993 in the brutal round of pit closures engineered by the Tories, its loss inflicted grievous economic and social damage on the local community. Dereliction and drug addiction, with heroin cheap as chips, added to the problem. Rows of terraced houses near to the former pit, where the heroin dealers operated, had to be demolished. The relatively high pay and solidarity of pit work was replaced by unemployment, low pay, short-term contracts or agency work in warehouses virtually bereft of union organisation.

A report by the Wakefield Poverty and Prosperity Commission, published in October 2012, highlighted the shocking levels of poverty in the former mining areas covered by the Wakefield Metropolitan District Council. (2) In Hemsworth and South Elmsall four areas - Kinsley, Moorthorpe, Westfield and the Holmsley Estate - were identified as 'priority areas' after they were found to be among the UK's most deprived 10 per cent. The report said the links between joblessness and early death were 'worryingly high' with people in the deprived areas living almost nine years less than those in the more affluent areas. The consequences of the pit closures, and the knock-on effects on engineering and a host of ancillary industries linked to mining are still with us and they are, literally, deadly. One resident quoted in the report highlights the struggle and constant grind of poverty and low pay:

> I don't want the high life, but I do want a decent life for me and my kids. I want to live without counting the pennies every week and without being nervous that I can't afford what's in my basket when I get to the checkout. I want to live without being scared of having no job, no money and no future.

Anyone who travels today in West Yorkshire around Castleford, Normanton or South Elmsall will see what replaced mining – huge warehousing depots with easy access to the M62, M1 and A1 routes to shift their goods. Many ex-miners, anxious for some sort of a job, passed their HGV licences to drive the lorries transporting the goods to and from the depots. Grey, prefabricated warehousing structures dominate the landscape and going onto the industrial estates most of the time is quite eerie. They are quiet places except when the lorries are loading and unloading; people aren't around, and, because the warehouses were built on cheap land away from the former mining towns and villages, to get to work in what are isolated areas, most people have to drive or use the buses. The only real sign of people is when the shifts change, normally at 6.00am, 2.00pm and 10pm.

Superdrug has a distribution centre on the huge Dale End warehousing complex between South Elmsall and Upton. The company, the UK's second largest health and beauty retailer after Boots, with 1,000 stores and 16,000 staff, is part of a worldwide conglomerate, Hutchison Whampoa of Hong Kong, with an annual turnover in excess of £10 billion. Three UK depots supply the stores scattered through the UK but the South Elmsall one was the only one with union recognition. The motive for the management offensive was crystal clear. As the strike started, the company issued a statement: "At the beginning of June we announced a review which was likely to result in proposals to realign terms and conditions of colleagues in our three distribution centres in Dunstable, Pontefract and Avonmouth. It is with regret that the union has chosen this course of action and we continue to be keen to reach a satisfactory conclusion to our consultations."

Whether it was 'realign' or 'harmonisation', the other smooth word management used in press statements, Superdrug's intention was to push down wages and working conditions at South Elmsall to those at the other non-union depots. The company wanted to impose drastic changes to pay and working condition, including abolishing unsocial hours shift payments which would leave some workers out of pocket by more than £2000 a year. The management also wanted the power to change and schedule shifts with only seven days' notice and to opt out of the 48-hour European Working Time Directive, designed to prevent employers from forcing workers into doing excessive hours.

It got worse. Management also wanted to change pension entitlements and cut sick pay. They presented an ultimatum – accept the new conditions or you will be sacked. It was management by diktat, clearly calculated to hit the workers at a vulnerable time in the run-up to Christmas.

From the summer announcement of the company's plans, and in the run-up to the dispute, UNITE recruited strongly. Out of 310 workers 280 were UNITE members and in October the union balloted them. 86% voted for strike action and the indefinite strike began on 3 November. The decision to go on indefinite strike was deliberate – it was the only strategy that could win. As one of the strike committee explained:

We...decided (it) had to be an all-out indefinite

strike.

We went all-out because we've got a massive warehouse in Dunstable. If we just did a 24 or 48 hour strike it would be very easy for the company to mobilise our workload down to Dunstable. With an all-out indefinite strike, Dunstable would struggle to get the work done.

It was basically strategic, but the strength and feeling was there as well, so we decided to withdraw our labour indefinitely. (3)

The trade union and community response in support of the strike was inspirational, with UNITE putting £10,000 into the strike fund. Braziers and barbecues were set up outside the gates and a week into the strike a caravan was provided by UNITE. A lively 24-hour picket stopped all activity at the depot with no lorries in or out and, with one exception, even the non-union workers did not cross the picket line.

A local butcher, Voddens, supplied meat for the picket barbecue, and workers at the other depots on the complex supplied wood for the braziers. The Del Monte depot across the road from the Superdrug depot supplied water and let the strikers use the toilets, and a stream of well-wishers and supporters turned up to express support, including Steve Tulley, the former NUM branch secretary at Frickley. The strikers were young and old, male and female and included 30 Polish workers who backed the strike.

There was a confident mood, summed up by one woman striker: "My husband was a miner on strike in 1984. We had two kids and, like everyone, I worried about paying the bills and everything else. Now I know that if we can survive 12 months out on strike then we can survive this. The community spirit during the Miners' Strike was fantastic. We've got that spirit shining through today."

Living a mile or so from the Superdrug depot meant that supporting the strike became almost a daily focus for me because the view was this could be a long, hard-fought struggle. But there was also clear determination to see it through. This was the assessment of one strike leader: "I think at first the mood among the workers was confident but a little bit anxious. We've not been on strike in 24 years. It was always going to take a little bit of time to settle in to the striking way of life. But straight after the first two or three days of the strike we felt comfortable, we felt strong, we felt united and we felt we could stay out as long as it took." (4)

I phoned Paul Routledge, the *Daily Mirror* columnist, to tell him about the strike but he was already on to it. Over in South Elmsall for a drink in the 'Brookie' with long-standing friends from Frickley Colliery, he got the story about the strike literally first-hand as it started. His piece supporting the Superdrug strikers, 'Striking a big blow for a nation bullied by bosses,' appeared on Friday 6 November. He pointed out that the Superdrug strikers were not pursuing 'militant pay claims' but were involved in a defensive action "triggered by high-handed bosses eager to exploit the recession. Work harder, for longer, on lower pay and on anti-social shifts, they say." (5) To get national newspaper coverage on day three of the strike was a real morale booster.

Support for the strikers from trade unions poured in from across the region and nationally. As well as UNITE regionally and nationally, the regional TUC, Unison, the NUT and my union, the NUJ, all supported the strike. My NUJ branch in Leeds immediately sent £100, and a bucket collection at our national conference in Southport, Lancs, raised £545.60. Pieces about the strike went out through activist lists like the National Shop Stewards network and, at events organised around the book *Shafted,* I distributed Superdrug strike leaflets and urged people to support the strike. One event in particular, a packed out meeting in the Working Class Library and Museum in Salford, on 20 November was memorable.

But the decisive factor which won the strike was the behaviour of the strikers, the confident way they organised themselves, and the way they stayed united. Mass meetings were held at the Moorthorpe Recreational Centre (the 'Rec') which was where the NUM strike committee met during the year-long strike. Amongst the men and women strikers were 20 former miners, and as one said to me, "I never thought I would be out on strike 25 years later." But he also said they had put into practice lessons learned during the strike – regular mass meetings and the active involvement of the strikers so that people didn't sit at home moping.

Steve Benn, the senior steward, and former Frickley Colliery miner, chaired the often boisterous meetings in a quiet, calm manner. Simon Coop, another younger shop steward, was an effective speaker who went out to address solidarity meetings and build support. But the two key factors which ensured success after three weeks on strike were, firstly, the absolutely solid picket of the South Elmsall depot which ensured nothing moved from it. The second factor was an imaginative tactic, a variation on the flying picket tactic, which involved strikers taking the message to Superdrug shoppers:

We sent out 28 cars - full to the brim with people - all over the country to hand out these leaflets, telling the public to support us by not shopping at Superdrug. We handed out nearly 125,000 leaflets about our campaign and we went to 140 towns and cities getting the message across.
The response was great. Obviously we were well received in traditional Labour areas. We were welcomed with open arms in the north east, in Lancashire and Yorkshire. Overall I'd say 85 percent

The Media, the Police & the Miners' Strike

of the public supported our campaign. (6)

The people on these 'flying consumer boycott pickets' were media savvy, making sure that, when they were in a town or city leafleting, they got the message into 33 local newspapers and on local radio.

The impact of all this activity had the management reeling as they recognised that perishable products, which should have been in Superdrug shops for the crucial Christmas season, were trapped inside the South Elmsall depot. One woman striker said, "I think the mice will have been having a party. There are lots of crisps, selection boxes and advent calendars. Who knows what damage the mice will have done?"

Paul Routledge did another piece in the *Mirror* on 20 November in which he renamed the company 'Supersack' when he revealed that dismissal notices had been sent out to the striking workers. He ended the piece pointing out that what the strike was about was "the difference between a living wage and living on benefits..."(7)

This piece appeared the same day that a deal was thrashed out after eight hours of talks at ACAS and on the following Monday the strikers voted by 185 to 59 to accept the offer. Steve Benn commented, 'We've done well. We got them to the table in three weeks. I thought it would take longer." Clearly a significant minority thought continuing the strike could have achieved more. One worker said, "I would have been happy to hold out for more and stay on the picket line, but we took a vote and the offer was accepted."

A union committee member made this assessment of the deal:

> I think the most important thing of all, which swayed the 76 percent of people to vote 'yes' to the deal, was that the common working practices we've had over the past 24 years will remain intact. There will be no annualised hours or flexibility. The

132

company will not be able to force anybody into doing something that they don't want to do.

We've lost big time on overtime payments. But overtime is only worked by the minority. We've gained 80 percent on what we lost before we walked out on strike, so as a union committee we feel that we can class this as a victory. I hope bosses now think twice about how they treat workers. Not just the bosses at Superdrug but also anywhere else with a union. The unions are there for a purpose and that was recognised. We struck and fought as one, and I would hope that would make bosses wary about tackling any other workforce, not just us. (8)

During the strike I began writing to prominent figures in the local area, asking them to send in messages of support to Superdrug, and received this from Ian Clayton on the day the vote was taken to return to work:

I am proud to send a message of support to the Superdrug strikers. I don't know, have never known, a man or woman who takes strike action without good reason, especially just before Christmas. It seems to me that the workers at Superdrug have every good reason and every right to be on strike and every right-minded person should get behind their struggle.

I hereby promise to boycott all Superdrug products until the strike is resolved to the satisfaction of union members and to advise all my friends to do the same. I shall also contribute financially to the strike fund and help in any other way I can.

In solidarity

Ian Clayton (Broadcaster and writer)

Featherstone West Yorkshire

Ian didn't need to follow up on his pledges, but it is one example of the powerful surge of support which pushed the Superdrug strikers to victory.

The return to work was also a poignant reminder of the different end to the 1984-85 miners' strike in March 1985 when the Frickley miners and their wives and supporters marched back behind their banner. At 5.30am on Tuesday 24 November 2009 Superdrug strikers assembled with their UNITE flags at the *Barnsley Oak* pub to march back to work to the depot, about half-a-mile away. As the strikers marched through the gate into the depot, celebratory rockets shot up and lit the dark night sky.

Notes

134

(1) The *Hemsworth and South Elmsall Express* is owned by Johnson Press, the fourth largest local and regional newspaper publisher. During the dispute the coverage in the local paper by Gemma Jimmison was exemplary. However Johnson Press revenues from advertising fell drastically during the recession and the company faced financial problems as a result of high levels of debt (over £300 m at the end of December 2013). Cost-cutting has closed the offices for two papers, the *Pontefract and Castleford Express* and the *Hemsworth and South Elmsall Express* based in the former mining communities. The journalists now work from the *Wakefield Express* office in Wakefield. This inevitably has an impact on the papers' content, with specific local news being replaced by general features. The future of local newspapers which play a key role in providing information to local communities as well as reporting and campaigning on local concern, is one of the big issues my union, the NUJ, is attempting to highlight.

(2) *http://www.wakefieldtogether.org.uk/PPC/default.htm*

(3) *Socialist Review*, Dec. 2009, 'Superdrug: The poor can't take it anymore'.

(4) ibid

(5) *http://www.mirror.co.uk/news/uk-news/superdrug-employees-are-striking-a-big-blow-429386*

(6) *Socialist Review*, Dec. 2009.

(7) *http://www.mirror.co.uk/news/uk-news/scrooge-is-alive-and-well-and-working-for-superdrug-432331#.UtrEz_JFAeg*

(8) *Socialist Review*, Dec. 2009.

THE TRUTH ABOUT OUR PIT CLOSURES

Letter to Pontefract and Castleford Express, 9 January 2014
    So we now know that there was a plan to wreck the
    coal-mining economy of the UK in 1984 and put
    nothing significant in its place in industrial Yorkshire.
    We also know that the planning for that confrontation
    dated back a year and was not the subject of debate in
    ministries, before parliamentary committees or on the
    floor of the commons.
    We now know that the miners' union was right when
    they said that 70 pits would quickly close and that such
    a move should be resisted. We also know that when
    MacGregor, the man in charge, sent letters to miners
    saying that he knew nothing of this, he was lying.
    The 1984-85 coal strike taught us all a number of
    lessons. One was that working men, and the women
    who supported them, get prison records for relatively
    minor misdemeanours when they seek to protect their
    livelihoods, but bankers who manipulate bank rates to
    their own advantage and cripple economies are
    reprimanded, apologise, and are not imprisoned.
    We also know that if you believe that it is better to buy
    in Russian coal than produce it, you are as foolish as

those who say 'we are all in this together'.
Also, if you sell the family silver of transport, civic
housing stock and essential social services onto the
businessmen, the social profits drop like a stone but
bonus culture flourishes.
Brian Lewis

From 1979 Brian Lewis was one of the leaders of an
arts cooperative called the Yorkshire Art Circus which
worked with artists, writers and theatre workers on a
number of projects which took the mining community as
their central theme.

"During the strike," he writes, "I was able to help a lot
of people create and generate their own books. YAC also
wanted to explore other ways that individuals and communities could communicate. Our Motto was Everybody
Has A Story To Tell. We Find Ways To Help Them Tell
Stories. Writing, photography, performance, banner-mak-
ing, music, poetry, community histories, political peg rugs
and painting were grist to the mill...To see the strike as all
doom, gloom and grief is a mistake. In many ways, it allowed a bonding together of communities across a region
which was not expected. There was a sense of purpose
which was at variance with the 'loadsamoney' 1980s, a
time for new experience and the throwing off of stultify-
ing conventions. For many people, the coal strike was a
chance to see places well beyond the fringes of their own
village. In a few cases it went as far as to cure illness.

One woman I met who had been housebound because
of agoraphobia ended up addressing a meeting in Trafal-
gar Square. That was a dramatic case but you did not have
to go far to meet women who went to America, Russia,
and South American countries, Australia, New Zealand
and to almost all of the European Countries. Men also
travelled, but the impact of the women was decisive, and
a keen factor in keeping the community spirit alive." (1)

Note

(1) 'Organise, Educate, Agitate — A Political Artist's Experience of the Strike,' in *Digging the Seam: Popular Cultures of the 1984/5 Miners' Strike*, eds Simon Popple and Ian W. Macdonald. Oxford Scholars, 2012.

Contributors

JOHN BAILEY was a Fleet Street print worker, strongly associated with the right of reply, during the 1984-85 miners' strike. He was sacked, along with 6,000 other print and production workers, when Murdoch moved to Wapping in January 1986. He is on the National Council of the Campaign for Press and Broadcasting Freedom and a member of the News International Disputes Committee which organised the 25th anniversary exhibition of the Wapping dispute and the archive: *www. wapping-dispute.org.uk*

TONY HARCUP has worked as a staff and freelance journalist in both mainstream and alternative media, and at the time of the miners' strike he was a reporter for *Leeds Other Paper*. Tony remains an active member of the NUJ, and now teaches journalism at the University of Sheffield. His books include *The Ethical Journalist* (Sage, 2007), *Alternative Journalism, Alternative Voices* (Routledge, 2013), and *A Dictionary of Journalism* (Oxford University Press, 2014).

NICHOLAS JONES reported the 1984-85 miners' strike for BBC Radio. He was a BBC Industrial and Political Correspondent with the BBC from 1972-2002. His books include *Strikes and the Media* (1986) and most recently *The Lost Tribe: Whatever Happened to Fleet Street's Industrial Correspondents?* His reflections on the pit dispute and commentaries on Mrs Thatcher's cabinet papers relating to the strike can be accessed under trade union reporting at www.nicholasjones.org.uk

PETER LAZENBY has been a newspaper reporter in Yorkshire for 47 years. He is now Northern Reporter for the *Morning Star*, Britain's only national, daily, socialist newspaper.

JULIAN PETLEY was one of the authors of *Media Hits the Pits* (1985). He is Professor of Film and Television at Brunel University and chair of the Campaign for Press and Broadcasting Freedom.

RAY RILEY is a former NUM activist who worked at Frickley Colliery in South Elmsall, West Yorkshire. Since leaving the coal industry in 1989 Ray has worked in the voluntary sector for the past 18 years. He is married with 2 children one of whom was born during the 1984-85 strike. Ray is currently working on a book about the battle at Frickley Colliery in November 1984, which graphically details his own personal experiences of police brutality, places the strike in a wider political context, and describes the daily struggles and the effect the strike had on his wife and young family.

PAUL ROUTLEDGE is a *Daily Mirror* columnist and was previously political correspondent on *The Observer* and the *Independent on Sunday* and labour editor of *The Times*.

GRANVILLE WILLIAMS lives in the former mining area of West Yorkshire. He is the author of *Remembering How It Was: Mining in the Leeds Area* (1993) and editor of *Shafted: The Media, the Miners' Strike and the Aftermath* for the 25th anniversary of the strike in 2009. He is on the National Council of the Campaign for Press and Broadcasting Freedom.

Tony Harcup, Nicholas Jones, Peter Lazenby, Julian Petley and Paul Routledge all contributed to *Shafted: The Media, the Miners' Strike and the Aftermath* (2009).

Help us to be effective.
Join the **CPBF**

The CPBF was established in 1979 by people - mostly in the media unions - who wanted to resist the power of the corporate press and campaign for the real independence and accountability of the media.

In 1995 Tony Blair decided that the support of Rupert Murdoch was crucial to electoral success and Labour abandoned long-standing policies on media ownership. The CPBF became a lone voice challenging the orthodoxies of deregulation and liberalisation of media ownership pursued by New Labour.

We saw the stark consequences of these policies in July 2011 when Murdoch's media empire, intent on acquiring full control of the enormously profitable BSkyB, was suddenly engulfed in the phone-hacking scandal. The crisis rocked the media, police and political establishment and led to the Leveson inquiry and report.

Now politicians are rediscovering the crucial link between a diverse media and a healthy democracy, and the need to place ownership limits on big media.

If you don't think we get the media we deserve, join with us to campaign for more diverse, democratic and accountable media. We are a membership-based organisation which relies on individuals and organisations for the funds to continue to do our work. You can find out more about us and download a membership form from: http://www.cpbf.org.uk
email us at freepress@cpbf.org.uk
or write to us at CPBF, 23 Orford
Road, Walthamstow, London E17 9NL